# IMAGING EDEN

Photographers Discover the Everglades

NORTON MUSEUM OF ART

Daylight

Cofounders: Taj Forer and Michael Itkoff
Designer: Ursula Damm
Copy editor: Elizabeth Bell

This publication accompanies the exhibition, *Imaging Eden: Photographers Discover the Everglades*, organized by the Norton Museum of Art (March 18–July 12, 2015).

The exhibition is made possible through the generosity of **Muriel and Ralph Saltzman** and
**William and Sarah Ross Soter**

With additional support provided by an award from the National Endowment for the Arts/Art Works, the William and Sarah Ross Soter Photography Fund, the Photography Committee of the Norton Museum of Art, and The Chastain Charitable Foundation.

With special thanks to The Everglades Foundation.

This publication is funded, in part, by a grant from the National Endowment for the Arts.

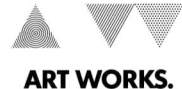

**ART WORKS.**

**National Endowment for the Arts**
arts.gov

Daylight Books
E-mail: info@daylightbooks.org
Web: www.daylightbooks.org

# TABLE OF CONTENTS

# FOREWORD

With the mission of its founder in mind—preserving beauty and educating the public—the Norton is no stranger to using art and culture to foster dialogue about greater societal issues on a local, national, and even international scale.

It is fortuitous, therefore, when the subject of an exhibition has roots very close to home and also achieves a vastly broader reach. *Imaging Eden: Photographers Discover the Everglades* is such an exhibition. The Everglades is a unique ecosystem, and perhaps one of the most contested landscapes on the planet. It is also our backyard.

The Everglades originally comprised more than eight million acres of ecosystem that stretched from the Kissimmee River watershed through Lake Okeechobee and south to Florida Bay. It provides a home to more than 350 species of birds and 1,000 forms of plant life. Its protected regions shelter nearly 70 threatened or endangered species. UNESCO has twice added the Everglades to the list of World Heritage Sites in Danger. But for those of us who call South Florida home, it is also an engine for economic growth, fodder for political and social wrangling, and, on a more basic level, the source of our drinking water.

The Everglades has driven the formation and expansion of Florida's identity, prosperity, and growth. Through it all, photography—as well as the artists who use it—has played an important role in the construction of both its myth and reality. *Imaging Eden* is the first exhibition to examine this phenomenon from its 19th-century origins to its contemporary manifestations, and the Norton Museum of Art is proud to have organized it.

Hope Alswang
*Executive Director & CEO*
*Norton Museum of Art*

# INTRODUCTION

*by Scott Eyman*

Just as it suggested a new way of living, Florida demanded a new way of seeing—but it took a long time to get here.

The written record of the state begins in the 17th century; the movies came in the first decade of the 20th century, and they were quickly followed by millions of tourists seeking to escape winter's chill.

Photography took longer, perhaps because 19th-century photography largely derived from 18th- and 19th-century painting, with a premium put on majestic landscapes. The paintings of Caspar David Friedrich and

Frederic Edwin Church gave way to the photography of Eadweard Muybridge and Ansel Adams.

The traditional manner of layering visual images—foreground objects to set off the majestic mountains in the background—were useless with a landscape like Florida's, which is basically flat. As a result, the Everglades, the state's great geographical and spiritual treasure, remained largely unexamined for hundreds of years.

For that matter, there were only fragmentary sightings of Florida as a place to live and work

rather than visit, and for good reasons. Take, for example, *Jonathan Dickinson's Journal*, the true story of how, in 1696, a Quaker merchant was shipwrecked by a hurricane off what is now Jupiter Island. The local Indians burned and looted the wreck and took the castaways to their settlement at Jupiter Inlet, where they stripped them of most of their clothes, even as one of the Indian women nursed Dickinson's infant son.

The Indians eventually released Dickinson's party, whose members made their way to the Spanish colony at St. Augustine. After further adventures, and no small amount of mercy from a grudging Providence, Dickinson's party made it to Philadelphia, where he eventually became mayor. Dickinson wrote of his adventures in a travelogue published in 1699.

The moral of the story hasn't changed in over 300 years: the natives of Florida are unpredictable when they're not downright dangerous.

As late as 1900, the population for the entire state was only 529,000 people. By 1920, it had grown by 52 percent, and by the end of the decade it had increased to 1.46 million, thanks in large part to Henry Flagler, the cofounder of Standard Oil, who transformed St. Augustine into something resembling Newport.

For his next trick, he extended the rail line south along the coast to Palm Beach, then all the way to Land's End: Key West. Along the

way, Flagler built a new town for the servants of the wealthy called West Palm Beach. Joseph Jefferson, the 19th-century actor famed for his portrayal of Rip Van Winkle, became a large landowner in West Palm Beach, and owned the town's first electric plant, as well as six houses and the Jefferson Hotel on Clematis Street.

The infrastructure built by Flagler enabled the land boom of 1924–25, attracting multitudes hungry for fortune—or just something easier than what they already knew. "For the first time in the national life," said historian George Mowry, "masses of Americans sought not opportunity but indulgence." [1]

In Dade County, the assessed property values mushroomed from $63.8 million in 1922 to

$421 million in 1926. Carl Fisher, who had previously devised the Indianapolis Speedway, created Miami Beach out of a glorified sand spit, then became the driving force behind the Dixie Highway, a north–south artery that extended all the way to Chicago. Frederick Lewis Allen wrote that "the whole strip of coast line from Palm Beach southward was being developed into an American Riviera . . . in fifty-foot lots." [2]

What Flagler had wrought Addison Mizner decorated, creating an echt-Meditteranean style that became the prevailing aesthetic in Palm Beach. Mizner was part genius, part con man, and he saw no reason why he should stop with architecture. He visualized Boca Raton as featuring a "Venetian canal" with motorized gondolas, a grand hotel, an airport, golf courses, and a yacht basin. Behind the scenes, Mizner's publicist admitted that it was actually being built to serve as "a platinum sucker trap."[3]

The developers dredged and built, the public came, and gold rush legends were born. One man picked up some ocean frontage for 25 cents an acre and sold it for a million dollars; a returning soldier traded his overcoat for 10 acres near the beach and sold it for $25,000. A pretty brunette who had been recently widowed talked about what Florida meant to her: "Came with a special party two weeks ago. Bought the third day. Invested everything. They guarantee I'll double by February. Madly absorbing place. My husband died three weeks ago. I nursed him over a year with cancer. *Yet I've actually forgotten I ever had a husband. And I loved him, too, at that.*"[4]

Were the stories true? Probably. Did it matter? Probably not.

While all this was going on, the literary and theatrical elites of New York and Hollywood were flooding into Palm Beach every winter. Irving Berlin, Joseph Schenck, and passels of movie stars from Gloria Swanson on down were all ensconced at the Breakers on a regular basis. But there is no record that any of them crossed the bridge to West Palm Beach, let alone drove the 116 miles to the Everglades. Their idea of the wild was the Junglewalk, a semi-wild trail in Palm Beach traversed by wicker vehicles pushed by black servants— hence the term Afromobiles.

Legions of the wealthy and privileged arrived around Christmas and went back to New York by Easter to write Broadway plays and movies about the place: *The Coconuts* (1929), starring the Marx Brothers; *The Palm Beach Girl* (1926), a silent film shot in and around the Breakers that unfortunately has been lost. America began to think of South Florida as an exotic equivalent of the French Riviera, but without the expense and downtime of an ocean voyage.

But the air began to leak out of the land bubble in 1926, the hurricanes of 1926 and 1928 and the Stock Market crash of 1929 put paid to the fantastic appreciation. Nevertheless, Florida had begun to stake its claim on the imagination of the American public.

Writers who didn't bear the class prejudices of the New York contingent began filtering in to Florida, not to visit but to live—there was a

Depression on, and Florida was cheap. For the most part, they liked what they saw. Marjorie Kinnan Rawlings's memoir *Cross Creek* (1942), attentive and respectful to the details of the cracker life, and ecstatically written, was predicated on the already evident fact that something about the farthest quadrant of America attracted those in need of a new life.

*Cross Creek* was an enlargement of Rawlings's *The Yearling* (1938), her famous novel about a 19th-century Florida farming family struggling to survive while a boy raises a pet deer and becomes a man, all too abruptly. It won the Pulitzer Prize.

What Rawlings did for Florida's rural whites, Zora Neale Hurston did for Florida's rural blacks. *Their Eyes Were Watching God*,

Hurston's 1937 novel, is aflame with a passionate attention to the behavior, language, and sociology of the black population that America at large ignored for nearly a century after the Emancipation Proclamation. It's the great novel of the Harlem Renaissance that just happens to take place in central Florida.

Ernest Hemingway had made his home in Key West since 1929, largely because it was a down-at-the-heels Cuban fishing village where he could be left alone to concentrate on his writing and drinking. Besides that, it was close to his beloved Gulf Stream.

He finally got around to writing about Florida in *To Have and Have Not*, published in 1937. It was a pure Hemingway product, especially in its studied belligerence — Hemingway loved to use

fiction to take revenge on his inferiors, imagined or actual. The primary victim of *To Have and Have Not* was John Dos Passos, who was brutally satirized as the sexually impotent phony radical Richard Gordon. More broadly, the novel portrayed Key West as a haven for third-stage drunks, has-beens and never-wases — a place for last chances that became the pattern for writers as varied as Thomas Sanchez and Carl Hiaasen well into the 21st century.

It was Marjorie Stoneman Douglas who asserted that the Everglades, and by extension all of wild Florida, was a work of art by the greatest artist of them all. Douglas's *River of Grass* was published in 1947 and has never been out of print, serving as a call to battle for generations on behalf of the greatest of Florida's wild places.

Douglas aside, fiction and nonfiction about Florida were roughly analogous to Willa Cather's closely observed novels about Nebraska pioneers: books about people who were so far off the grid they might as well have been living on Easter Island. Which also described movies that were made here. Before World War I, the movie business was centered in New York, and Florida's ace in the hole was its climate. To get out of the horrible winters and maintain a steady level of movie production, early companies such as Kalem established Florida studios as early as 1908. Jacksonville was considerably more than a seasonal hub; more than 300 movies were made there between 1909 and 1926.

Florida as a movie studio was all well and good in the winter, but trying to shoot movies in the summer was impossible. If the mosquitoes didn't kill you, there was the heat, which would melt the emulsion on the film—literally. D.W. Griffith shot two films in and around the New River in Fort Lauderdale, but he had to work alfresco because there was no movie studio anywhere in the vicinity. As he wrote the Miami Chamber of Commerce in 1921, "Florida has a great many advantages in picture making, but primitive conditions there compared to the very modern facilities in California argue against Florida."

The primary stumbling block to living in Florida wasn't solved until air-conditioning became widely available just before World War II, which is when the Max Fleischer studios, the home of Betty Boop and Popeye, set up shop in Miami. Fleischer made two cartoon features and a series of shorts in Miami, in an operation that was meant to compete with Walt Disney's but didn't.

By that time, the movies had settled on using Florida as an exotic location rather than a production site. John Huston's *Key Largo* (1948) was an adaptation of a mildly successful Maxwell Anderson play about a group of dead-enders huddled together during a hurricane. Huston and his co-writer, Richard Brooks, spent some time in the Keys soaking up atmosphere while working on the screenplay, but the entirety of the film was made in Burbank. Glossy musicals such as *Moon Over Miami* (1941) utilized only second-unit footage of local landmarks, while the bulk of the film was made in Hollywood.

A few years later, that began to change. *Wind Across the Everglades* (1958), written by Budd Schulberg and directed (mostly) by Nicholas Ray, derived from some of the same legends that served as the background for Peter Matthiessen's Watson trilogy—avaricious outlaws operating an untouched empire of poaching and crime in the Everglades. It featured the head-spinning cast of Christopher Plummer, Burl Ives, Gypsy Rose Lee, and Emmett Kelly sans clown makeup. The film was shot entirely in Everglades City and Everglades National Park, but Nicholas Ray disappeared before it was completed, and in any case the movie was a commercial disaster.

Frank Sinatra was always good for work in Florida, in movies as varied as *A Hole in the Head* (1959), *Tony Rome* (1967), and *Lady in Cement* (1968). Sinatra liked shooting in Florida because he could double-dip—shoot his movie during the day and work in nightclubs after dark. Also serving as a goodwill ambassador was Jackie Gleason, who refused to broadcast his TV shows from anywhere but Florida for decades, each broadcast being heralded as emanating from Miami Beach, "the sun and fun capital of the world."

Central Florida was culturally electrified by the arrival of Disney World in 1971, which served to introduce the state to tens of millons, many of whom might never have visited otherwise, including many who made mental notes to come back—and, perhaps, live—as soon as possible.

Traditionally, the people who emigrated to South Florida were from New York and other East Coast points. But the continuing influx of Cubans in the wake of Castro irrevocably changed the nature of the state. By the early 1980s, a sign in a Miami Beach shop nicely captured the schizoid nature of South Florida: SE HABLA YIDDISH.

But that all changed with the influx of the fashion industry and the impact of *Miami Vice*—a confluence of style, money, and quantity of population constituting the critical mass that can leverage a city to the highest level.

Suddenly, South Florida was something besides God's Waiting Room or a vacation destination. Now it was hip to be in Florida, although still potentially dangerous. Witness Brian De Palma's *Scarface* (1983), a highly influential gangster movie about the glamour of violence, whose primary innovation was to convert the Italian gangster of Howard Hawks's 1932 original into a Marielito who turns to crime as a means of social assertion. *Scarface* had been preceded by *Body Heat* (1981), a variation on *Double Indemnity* that specifically utilized the sultry environment of South Florida as a corollary to its sexually overheated characters. The combination of sex, violence, and glamour has continued to define South Florida ever since.

If literature and movies circled around Florida with regularity before finally establishing a viable beachhead, television saw buried treasure and staked its claim on the region, especially the Everglades, early on.

From 1961 to 1962, character actor and outdoorsman Ron Hayes patrolled the exotic locations of south Florlda in his airboat as Constable Lincoln Vail in the Ivan Tors series *The Everglades!* Over the next decade, Tors's productions set in the Everglades would include the inimitable *Flipper* (1964–67) and *Gentle Ben* (1967–69), which made Lassie-like stars of a dolphin and a bear, respectively.

What becomes clear from this brief history is that the idea of Florida is continuously evolving to conform to the vision of creative people in all of the arts who came, saw, and were conquered by the state and its offbeat beauty.

---

1 Maury Klein. *The Crash of 1929* (New York: Oxford University Press, 2001), p. 88.
2 Klein, p. 92.
3 Klein, p. 92.
4 Klein, p. 94.

*Scott Eyman was the literary critic for the Palm Beach Post for 25 years. He has written 13 books, among them several* New York Times *best sellers, most recently* John Wayne: The Life and Legend.

# IMAGING EDEN:
## Photographers Discover the Everglades

*Tim B. Wride, William and Sarah Ross Soter Curator of Photography*

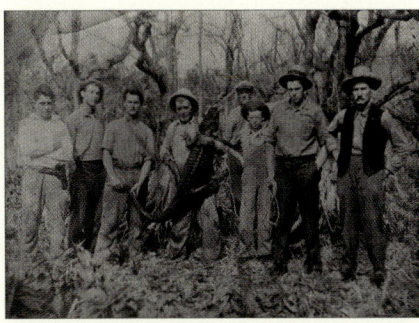

Unidentified Photographer
[Group portrait with alligator], 1916–1917

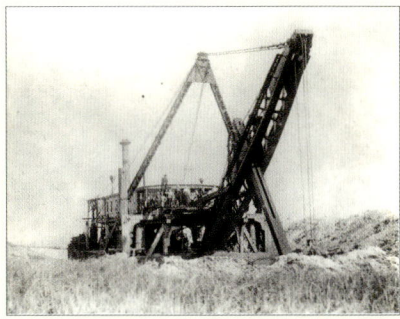

Unidentified Photographer
[Dredge, Okeechobee], 1908

The Everglades, as both place and idea, remains one of the last great expanses of unknown landscape in the nation. Taken at its most inclusive, the Everglades is an interconnected system of multiple environments that stretch from the Kissimmee River watershed through Lake Okeechobee to Marjorie Stoneman Douglas's "River of Grass" before passing through what we know today as Everglades National Park and emptying into Florida Bay. In all, the system impacts, directly and indirectly, roughly two-thirds of the state of Florida. It has international, national, and local implications that can be measured beyond environmental, political, cultural, or socioeconomic scales.

From the beginning, the Everglades has driven the formation and expansion of the Caribbean and, specifically, Florida's identity, prosperity, and growth. The landscape readily became a battleground between environmental reality and economic potential. Within days of Florida's admission to the Union as the 27th State in 1845, Congressional discussions were being held to initiate a large-scale drainage of the Everglades to accommodate population growth and agriculture. The last half of the 19th century saw repeated military campaigns to purge the region of its native and escaped-slave populations; land speculation schemes in the first half of the 1900s signaled cycles of boom and bust; and reclaimed Everglades

land became the exemplar of the postwar American Dream.

To all of this, and contrary to nearly every other example of geographic expansion and development in the nation's history, photography bore scant witness. Carleton Watkins had photographed Yosemite and the Pacific Northwest by the middle of the 1860s; William Henry Jackson photographed what would become Yellowstone National Park in 1871; and the same year, Timothy O'Sullivan made the first photographs of the Grand Canyon. And yet the Everglades was never systematically imaged until the 20th century. In spite of this relative image scarcity, photography

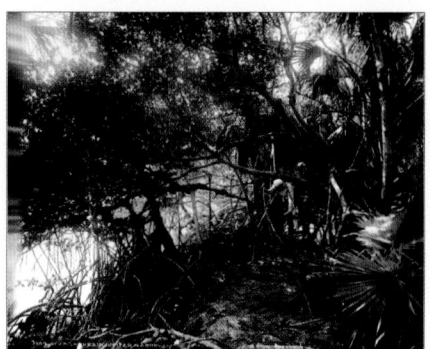

Wm. H. Jackson, *Mangroves in Jupiter Narrrows*, circa 1889

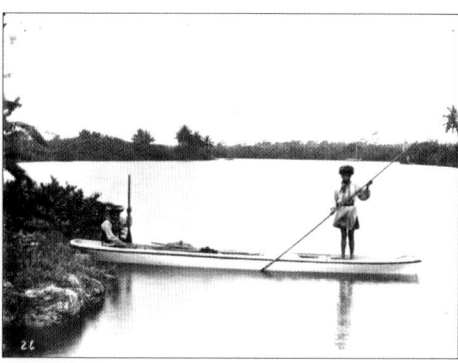

Ralph M. Munroe, *Ye Noble Red Men, Seminoles*, circa 1890

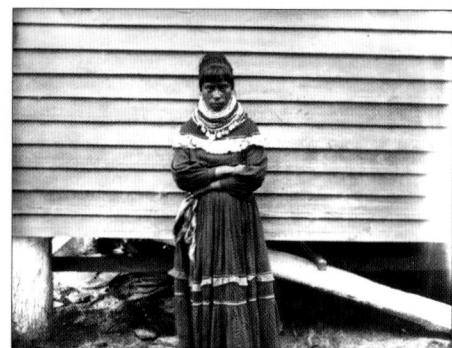

Ralph M. Munroe, *Cypress Charlie's Squaw, Seminole Indian*, circa 1890

has played, and continues to play, an important role in the construction of the myth and reality of the Everglades. The medium has alternately been silent witness, premeditated booster, relentless critic, and passionate advocate of this unique environment.

The photographic record that dates to the 19th and early 20th centuries consists primarily of what we now call vernacular imagery: picture albums that were kept by the pioneering families who sought to eke a life out in the newly reclaimed lands of the Everglades. It must be remembered that Kodak introduced the possibility of consumer photography with their mass-market camera in 1888, and so the Florida pioneers had the means to record their own histories as well as the history of the region.

Images of outings and special occasions are interspersed with impressive visual celebrations of massive sculptural dredgers and diggers busily draining the land; proud growers preen in front of towering crops, women pose before newly built homes; adolescent boys and men flaunt their dominance over the land and its creatures.

It cannot be said that there were not more serious photographs being taken in Florida. It is simply that they were, as a rule, not being taken in the Everglades. Celebrated photographer and publisher William Henry Jackson was in Florida on three separate occasions, and while most of his work was done in the north, there is a suite of images taken on a southerly steamer expedition that found him on the eastern doorstep of the Everglades in Jupiter and as

far south as Lake Worth. His images and those undertaken by others under contract to him were part of a visual record that was available through the W. M. Jackson Publishing Co. and then the Detroit Publishing Co.

Ralph Middleton ("Commodore") Munroe became a Florida resident in 1890 and meticulously, and with some talent, recorded his impressions of his new home. The land and its people were both exciting and exotic. Over a decade before Edward Sheriff Curtis was to begin his monumental ethnographic study *The North American Indian*, Munroe had begun to record the Seminoles of the region. It should be noted that Curtis only had contact with the Seminoles on their relocation lands in Oklahoma and never photographed in Florida.

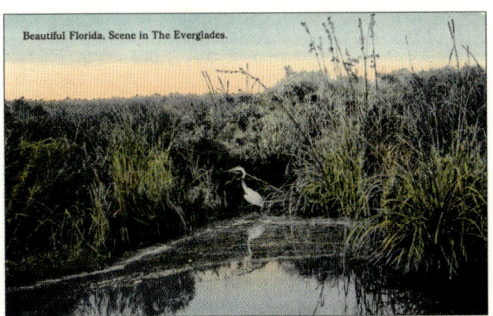

Postcard, circa 1920

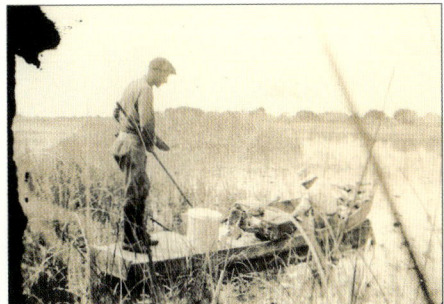

John King Sr., [In the glades], 1917

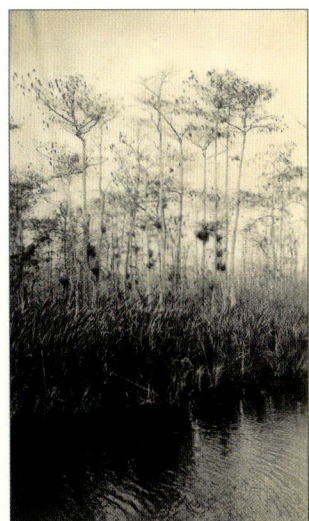

John King Sr., [Dense foliage], 1917

Munroe's images of the Seminoles, while posed in the sense that both photographer and sitter seem to take equal responsibility for the image, do not seem to have the theatricality that punctuate Curtis's studies.

One of the more impressive, though perhaps least-known, photographic undertakings within the Everglades region, however, was accomplished by John King Sr. along with his son, John Jr., and a youthful William Catlow. What started out as an excursion to survey two remote plots of land devolved into almost a month of wandering lost in the Everglades. The drama played out as it was happening in national newspapers, and after the fact graced the pages of the Audubon Society's magazine, *Forest and Stream*, accompanied by the party's photographs of the ordeal.

Magazines and journals became instrumental in posting a visual record for the region. In addition to the outdoor recreation journals (of which *Forest and Stream* was the first), the importance of the *National Geographic Magazine* cannot be overstated. On the pages of what was perhaps the most revered journal of the time, the Everglades and its wildlife, plant life, and way of life were portrayed with regularity beginning in 1896.

However, if there were a single most effective way in which an identity for South Florida and the Everglades was forged on a national and international stage, it would be through tourism and the production and dissemination of the picture postcard. The most insidious of visual ambassadors, postcards carried

images of dubious veracity made credible by the acquaintance, friend, or loved one whose inscription it also delivered. Alligators, most often man-eating and monstrous, were common fare, and the exotic bird life as well as the alien dress and customs of the Seminoles were shamelessly exploited and cemented into the global consciousness. Yet the overriding beauty and captivating vistas of the place itself were most often the subject of the picture postcard. For, above all, the Everglades is a devastatingly memorable landscape.

Walker Evans is the undisputed master in the seemingly neutral depiction of the Southern experience. While he had visited Florida before, he did not experience the Everglades until 1941, when he accepted a commission from author

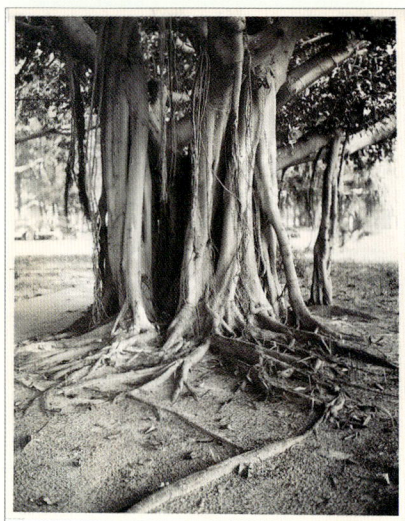

Walker Evans, *Banyan Tree*, Florida, 1941
©Walker Evans Archive, The Metropolitan Museum of Art

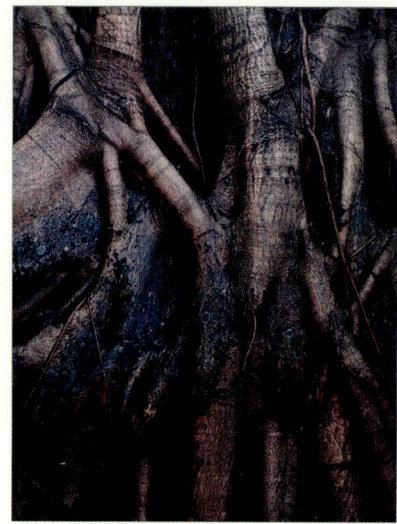

Eliot Porter, *Strangler Fig Roots*, 1954
©1990 Amon Carter Museum of American Art, Fort Worth, Texas

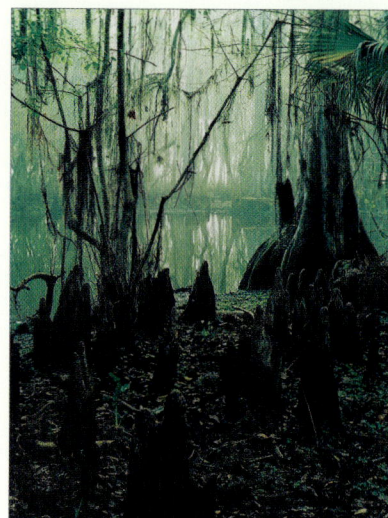

Eliot Porter, *Cypress Slough and Mist*, 1974
©1990 Amon Carter Museum of American Art, Fort Worth, Texas

and retired newspaperman Karl Bickel. Bickel commissioned Evans to illustrate his volume of the history and lore of Florida's western shore, *The Mangrove Coast*. The book awkwardly paired a suite of 31 Evans images with Bickel's text. Rarely do the two seem remotely complementary. Of the few images of "nature" that are included—a subject that Evans found none too interesting—the most arresting depict tortured palms at the shoreline and a sculptural-looking trunk of a banyan tree. The commission situated Evans in a region that had been largely ignored in favor of its more glamorous eastern cousin; it also put him at the edge of the Everglades.

Whether a potential part of the commission or out of sheer curiosity, Evans made an excursion by boat into the western reaches of the Everglades. Evans's negatives that he made during this outing carry a shadowed and somber emotion that one rarely associates with his work. His visual record of the day includes a suite of what can only be called abstractions that record the fleeting reflections of light across slow-moving dark water. Because they were never printed, it would be reckless to consider them part of the photographer's oeuvre. Yet what cannot be overlooked is the visual fascination and moody allure they depict. The place itself, with all of its subtleties and introspective opportunities, was clearly not lost on Evans. It was a landscape like none other, and his reaction to it evinced an unexpected sensibility.

Following in the footsteps of artists who have exhibited a fascination with the Everglades as pure landscape, photographers have turned to the Everglades as a site of inspiration and commentary, and claimed the place as uniquely their own. While some have brought to their enterprise the strategies of the past and the traditional tropes of composition and spatial rendering, many approach this unique landscape on its own terms with an eye that less transcriptive than interpretive.

Eliot Porter was a master colorist. Like the work of most of his contemporaries, his photographs bear the hallmarks of an artist for whom situation is crucial. Yet his ability to capture a moment in time is always coupled with the need to orchestrate hue and color to an expressive end. His choice of landscape as subject, however, set him apart from most

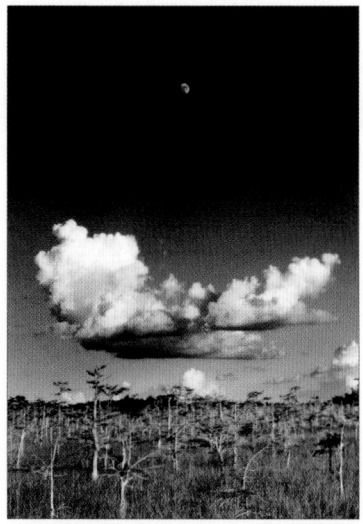

Clyde Butcher, *Moonrise Number Two*, 1986
© Clyde Butcher

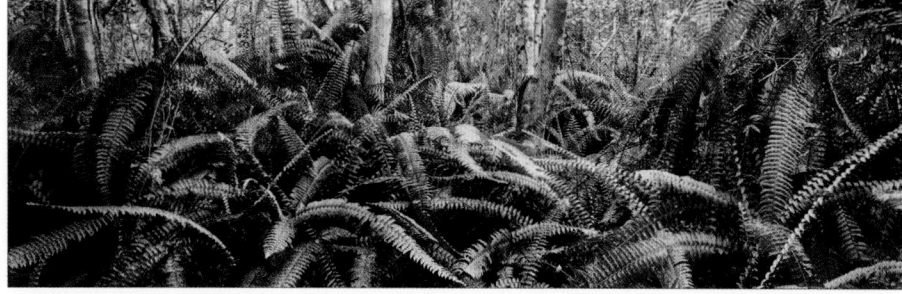

Mary Peck, *Everglades*, 1988

of the more celebrated photographers using color in his generation, such as Stephen Shore, William Eggleston, or William Christenberry. In the 1960s and '70s when Porter was making pictures in the Everglades, landscape photography was almost by definition a black-and-white enterprise. For art photographers and the curatorial world, color images of nature were too near an exercise in literal transcription than they were creative expression. Yet Porter's quiet sensibility, along with his sense of color, was perfectly suited to the restrained shifts of light and tone he encountered in South Florida.

If there is a classical black-and-white edenic approach to the Everglades, it is found in the work of Clyde Butcher. Adhering to

pictorial renderings that have their roots in the Hudson River School and following the photographic tradition of his early mentor Ansel Adams, Butcher manages to find the beauty of the place on its own terms. Adams and other practitioners of the Great American Landscape tradition such as John Sexton were afforded the luxury of approaching vistas that were both familiar and majestic. Butcher, however, ekes out his awe-inspiring and often sublime images from a landscape that is more understated than bombastic, more introspective than imposing, and more alien than august. Exploiting textures, highlights, and reflections, Butcher provides access to a different kind of nature that only the Everglades can offer, in a luminescent palette of black, grays, and white.

New Mexico artist Mary Peck also stems from the long tradition of black-and-white landscape photography. Like Butcher's, her images are sensitively rendered with a meticulous organization of visual elements and show masterful darkroom dexterity. Yet, that is where the similarity ends. Peck's experience of the Everglades is more mythic and internal. Her images are most often compressed to the front of the picture plane; they are a study in an exquisitely organized chaos, and they completely fill the frame. For Peck, the Everglades is unknowable, shifting, and mysterious—a site of catharsis, transmutation, and change. Peck's Everglades is at once physical and psychological. She seeks to celebrate what remains of the wild and untamed in a managed and domesticated world.

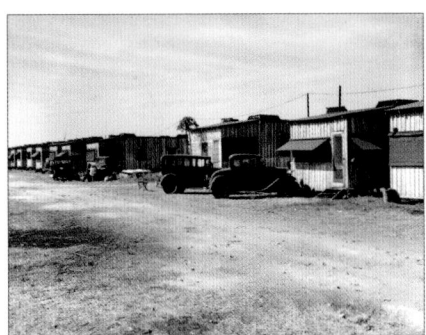

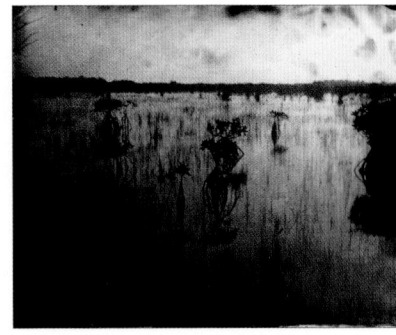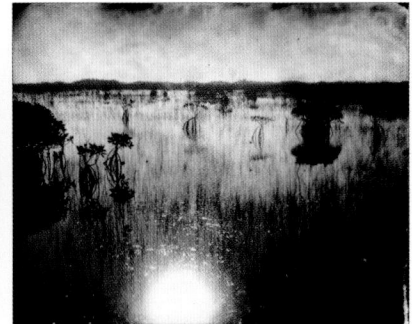

Marion Post Wolcott, *Migratory Workers'*

Lisa Elmaleh, *Mangroves*, 2010

Lisa Elmaleh is a native Floridian. As she tells it, her childhood was punctuated by trips into the Everglades with her father. As a photographer, however, it was not until her relocation to New York to study photography that she found both the means and the sensibility to render her experience of her childhood environment.

Elmaleh is one of a new generation of image makers who are looking back to 19th-century photographic processes—carelessly known today as "alternative processes." Unlike many, however, she has been able to seamlessly and authoritatively merge early analog techniques with her subjects in a manner that is thoroughly contemporary. Elmaleh chose to approach the Everglades using the same wet-plate collodion process that Carleton Watkins used in Yosemite and had a portable darkroom and lab outfitted onto the back of her truck. Her Everglades images seem to respond to the absence of any early surveyor work. Yet the moody and often scarred images are a confluence of the limitations of 19th-century process with the artist's juvenile memory and her modern image sensibility. They reach back in time and yet are purely contemporary.

For many photographers who have discovered the Everglades, however, the experience is more than just the landscape. To many of them, the place was, and continues to be, as much about the wildlife, the people, the history, and the way of life the place supports as it is about the terrain. This alternate approach to the Everglades attracts a different kind of photographer, one whose strategies and sensibilities are more suited to a documentary ethic.

Marion Post Wolcott was the first woman hired by director Roy Stryker to work on a full-time basis with the photographic team of the Farm Securities Administration—one among Franklin Roosevelt's plethora of New Deal agencies. Her assignments took her around the country and eventually found her in the shadow of the southern rim of the Herbert Hoover Dike around Lake Okeechobee. The small town of Belle Glade, Florida, had been all but destroyed during the hurricane that swept across the state in 1928. In the aftermath of the devastation, the US Army Corp of Engineers

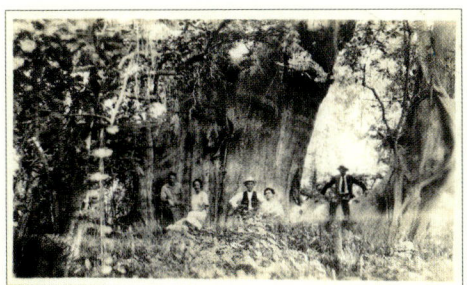

Unidentified Photographer, [Belle Glade], circa 1925

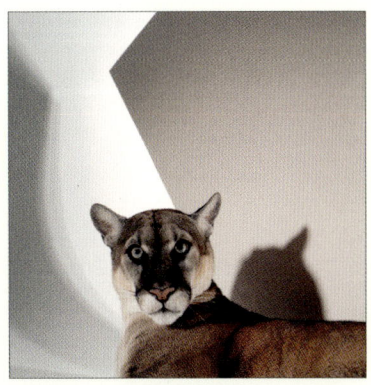

James Balog, *Florida Panther*, 1989
©James Balog/Aurora Photos

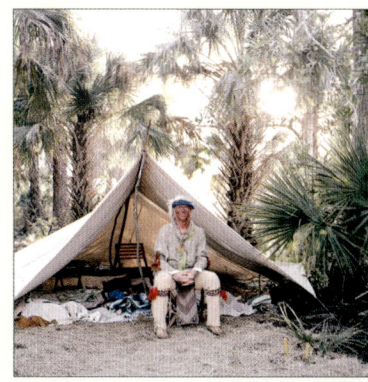

Adam Nadel, *Non-Native Seminole War Re-enactor*, 2014

was tasked to ring the lake with a dike as a means of flood protection for the communities and agricultural interests on its shores. While this was a successful answer to the problem in the short term, the project would have unforeseen long-range consequences.

Post Wolcott was sent to Belle Glade in 1939 and again in 1941 to document the situation and needs of the migrant farmworker population on whom the agricultural operations of the region depended. Her images pivot between the spartan short-term housing and daily existence of the nomadic workers and the more relaxed new attitude of the town seen in images of couples in the local speakeasy. In either case, her photographic approach to the Everglades—albeit a domesticated

Everglades—was driven by a programmatic and ideological purpose. This use of photography as a means of justifying policy or as visual proof of a thesis has become a staple for subsequent generations of photographers in their approach to the Everglades.

James Balog followed this strategy when photographing what were then endangered species from the Everglades and its subsidiary ecosystems in the late 1980s and '90s. More recently, Adam C. Nadel and Bryan Wilson each spent a month in residence at Everglades National Park as part of the Artists in Residence in the Everglades program. Both worked on projects that they had spent considerable time researching before their arrival, and both found that their study, while

extensive, did not prepare them for the reality of the places and situations they entered.

Nadel explains his project this way: *Getting the Water Right* tries to unravel the cultural, social, and economic forces that have led the Everglades ecosystem to the edge of disaster. Additionally, he seeks to reveal how these same forces are driving current restoration efforts. He says he is photographing the land, history, and people of Southern Florida to document how politics, culture, economy, and ecology have dynamically interacted, and often collided, to push the Everglades to the edge of unrecoverable collapse. The project is not only about the past, present, and future of one of the world's most unique ecosystems, it is also about future biodiversity on our planet.

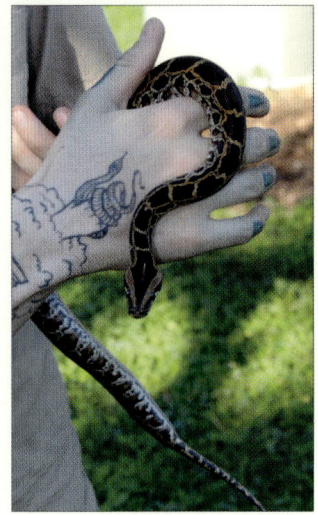

Bryan Wilson, *Double Snake*, 2013

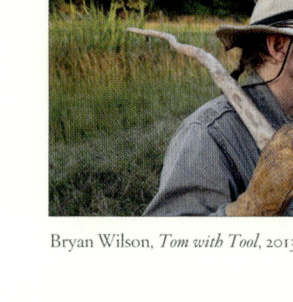

Bryan Wilson, *Tom with Tool*, 2013

His images range from abstractions of ocean and smoke to control rooms, pumping stations, and legislative meeting halls. The power of his project rests in the multiplicity of perspectives that he brings to bear on the issue. Nadel's project tackles a global issue from multiple regional perspectives.

Bryan Wilson, on the other hand, approaches a phenomenon—the proliferation of a non-native species, the Burmese python, in the Everglades—from a highly personalized perspective. As he defines his project:

*The Great American Python Project* is an artistic social investigation of the changing face of the Everglades National Park through the lens of invasive exotic species management. The Burmese Python (*Python bivittatus*) is one of many invasive exotic species thriving within South Florida, and the eradication of their populations seems untenable. Populations of Burmese Pythons are waning in their native habitats in South/Southeast Asia, posing the question: when does the Burmese Python become the American Python?

Wilson is affiliated with the Swamp Apes, whose core members are veterans of the wars in Iraq and Afghanistan and who are volunteers in Everglades National Park. With his new compatriots, Wilson helped clear pathways, capture pythons, and understand the ecosystem from a personal perspective. All the while he produced drawings, photographs, and patterns for textiles that documented his experience. His relationship with the Swamp Apes, as well as his production of art and artifacts based on his expansive understanding of the environment and its denizens, continues to evolve.

Photographers continue to discover the Everglades in their own ways and with their own sensibilities every day. They see truths and understandings of the place, its past, its potential, and its inhabitants. Their images and the stories they tell are both revelatory and prophetic. As artists have always done, they show us a part of our world and of ourselves that without them we would have missed.

# The Norton Everglades Commissions

WHEN RALPH H. NORTON BUILT THE COLLECTION THAT NOW
FORMS THE CORE OF THE MUSEUM BEARING HIS NAME, HE WAS
ADAMANT ABOUT WORKING WITH LIVING ARTISTS. WHEN HE
BUILT THE MUSEUM THAT WOULD HOUSE HIS COLLECTION IN
THE COMMUNITY OF WEST PALM BEACH, HE COMMISSIONED
ARTISTS TO PRODUCE WORKS THAT WOULD BE AN INTEGRAL
PART OF THE OVERALL PLAN. IN KEEPING WITH THE SPIRIT
OF MR. NORTON'S TRUST AND INTEREST IN THE WORKS OF
HIS TIME, IT HAS ALWAYS PART OF THE IDEA OF *IMAGINING
EDEN* TO COMMISSION CONTEMPORARY ARTISTS—ARTISTS
OF *OUR* TIME—TO DISCOVER THE UNIQUE ENVIRONMENTS
AND EXPERIENCES OF THE EVERGLADES ON THEIR OWN TERMS
AND FROM THEIR OWN PERSPECTIVES.

# JUNGJIN LEE

# Jungjin Lee

KOREAN-BORN ARTIST JUNGJIN LEE IS
KNOWN FOR HER METICULOUSLY RENDERED
REDUCTIVE LAND- AND WATERSCAPES AS
WELL AS FOR AN APPROACH TO OBJECTS
AND SITUATIONS THAT IS BOTH INTUITIVE
AND ELEGANT. SHE IS DRAWN TO SUBJECTS
THAT CARRY A PHYSICAL AS WELL AS A
PSYCHIC POTENCY. SHE HAS REMARKED THAT
HER EXPERIENCE OF PHOTOGRAPHING IN
THE EVERGLADES REQUIRED HER "TO SEE
DIFFERENTLY . . . FROM ABOVE AS IF A BIRD,
AND FROM BELOW AS IF A SNAKE."

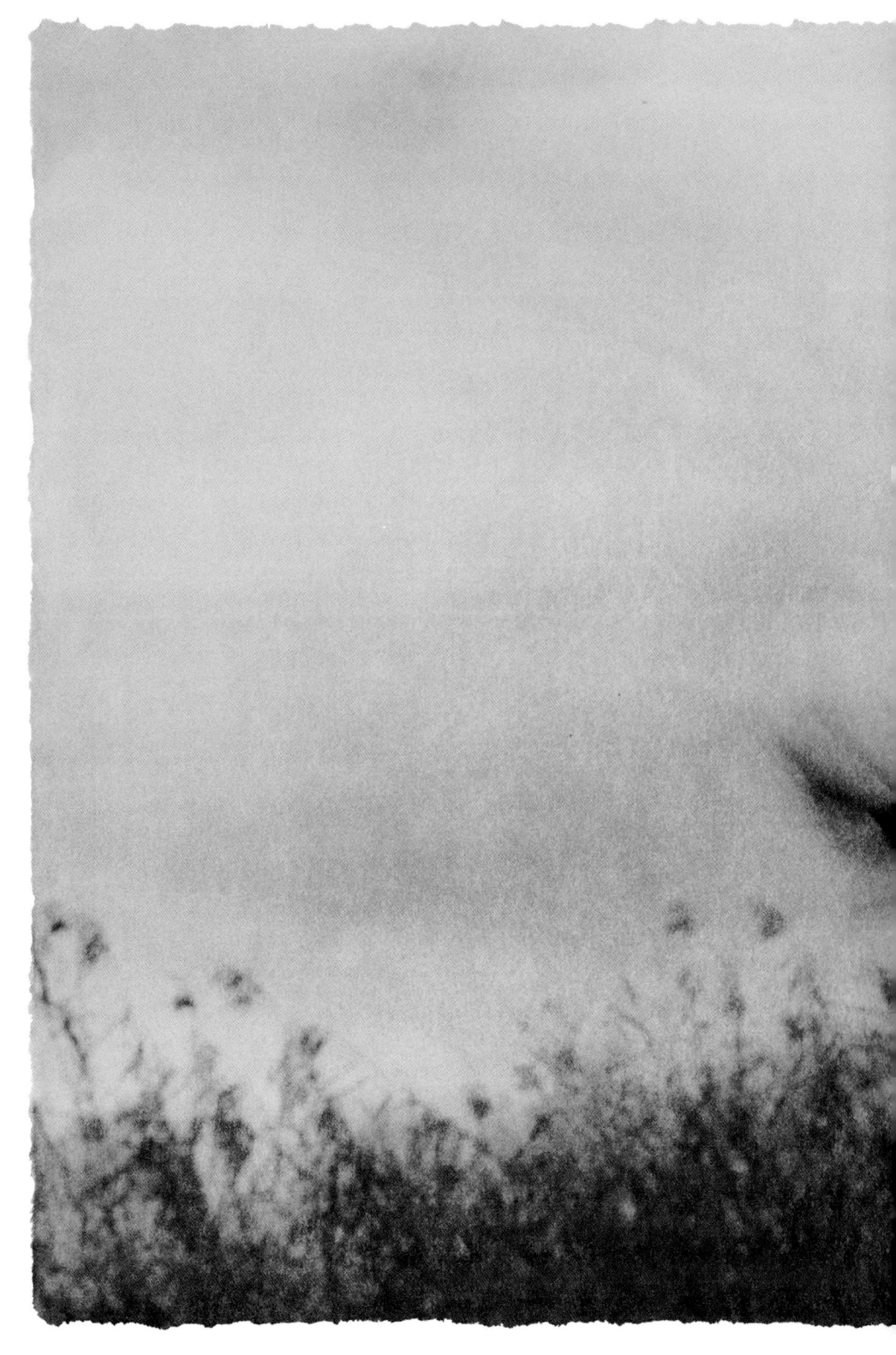

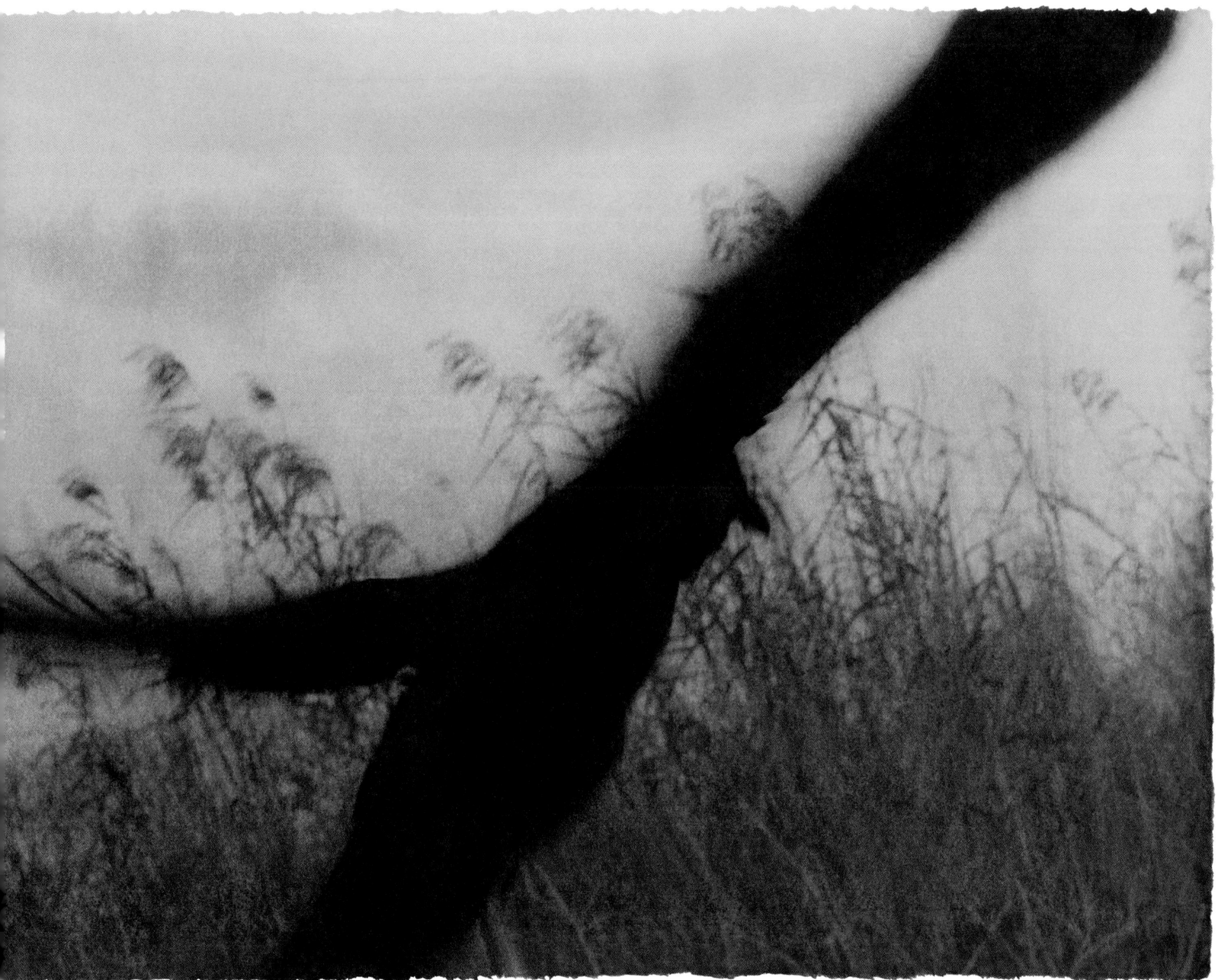

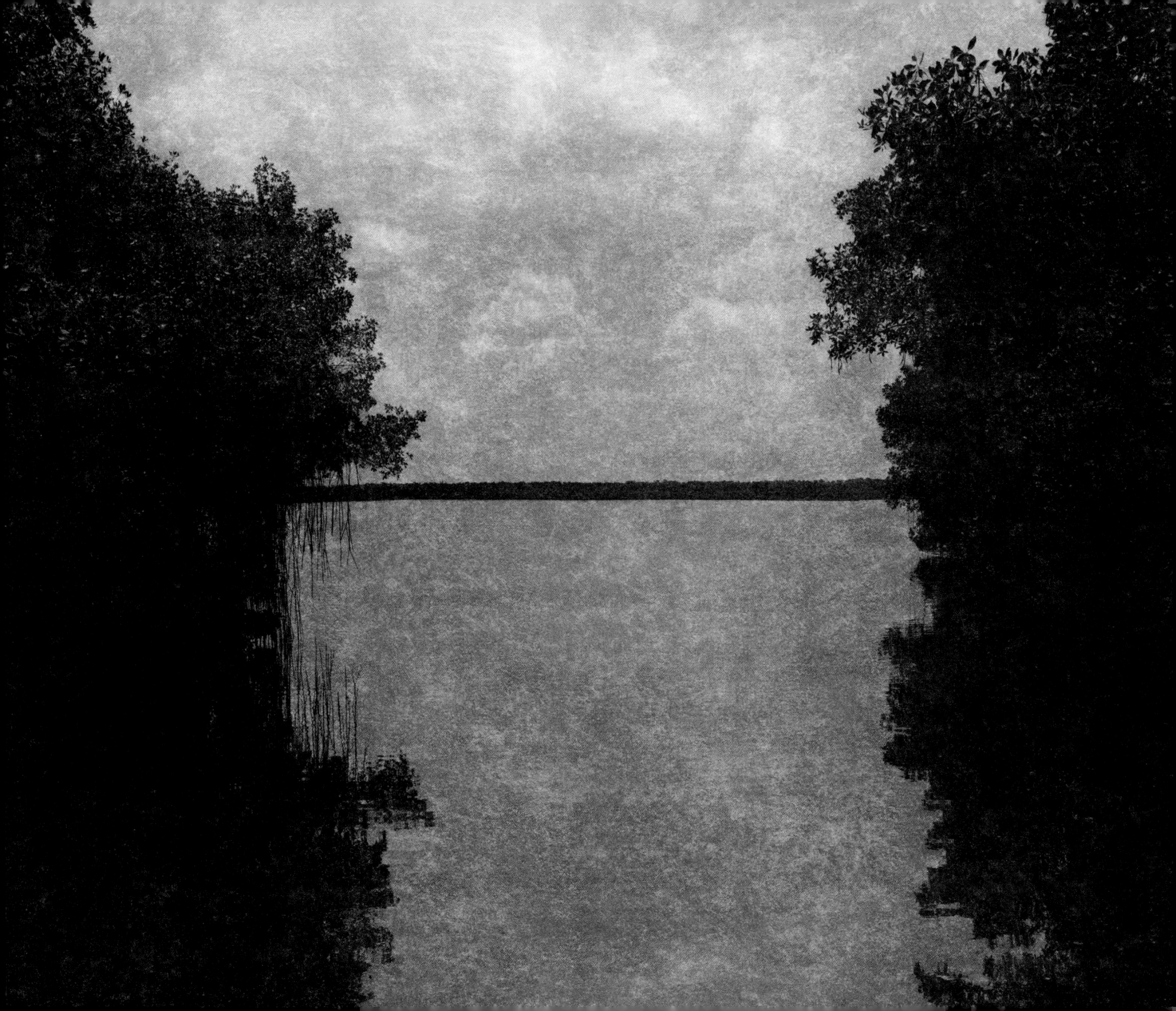

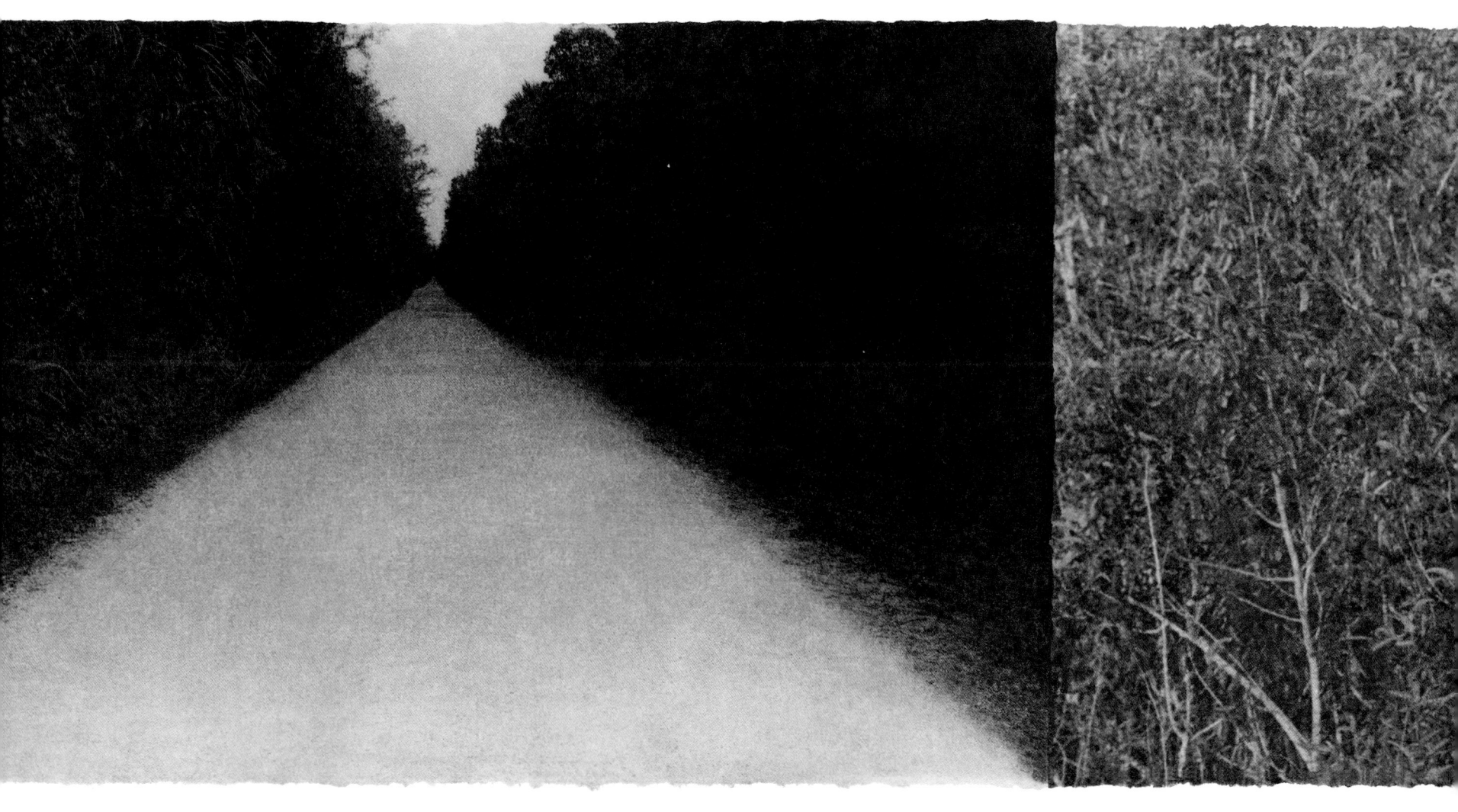

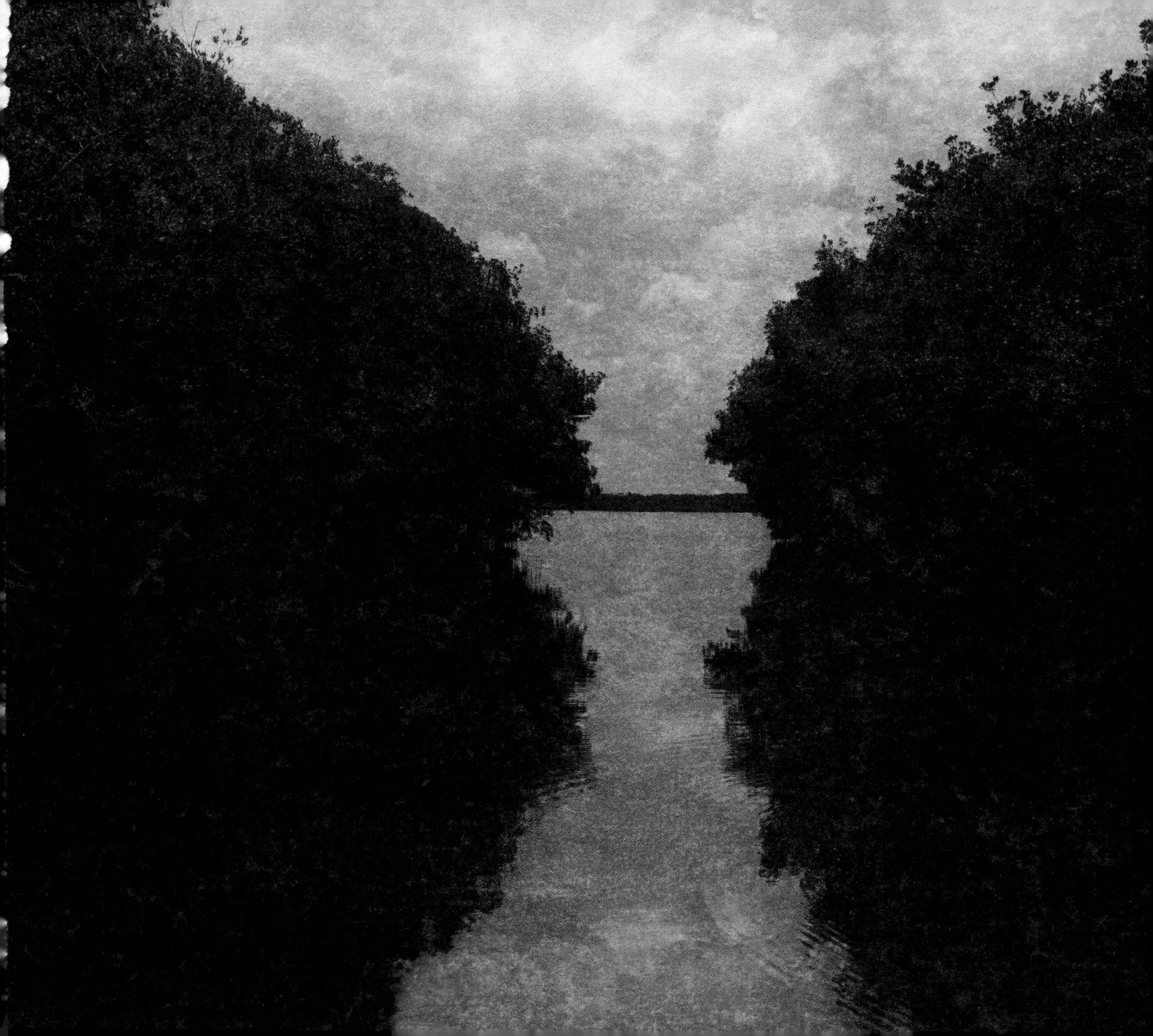

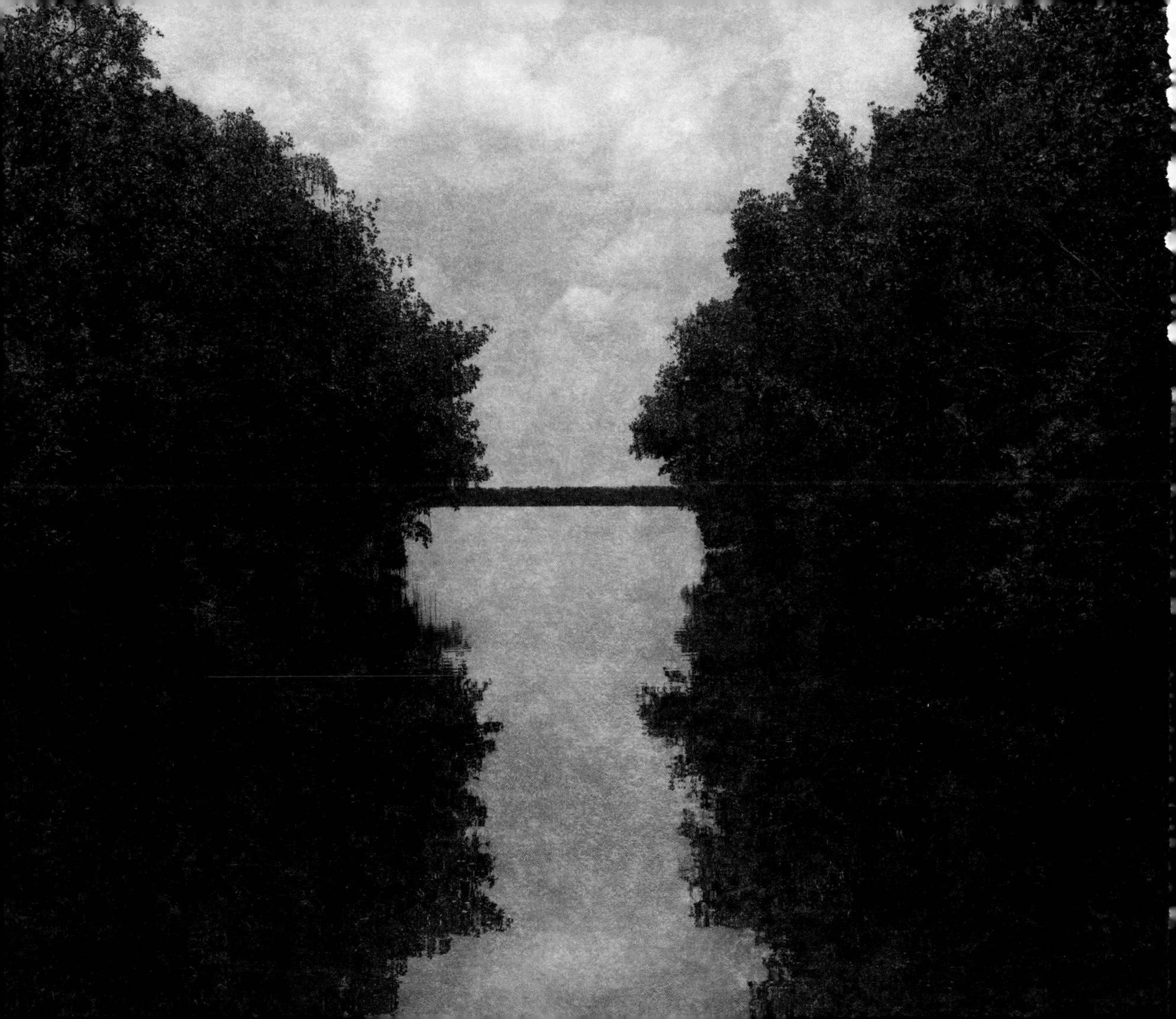

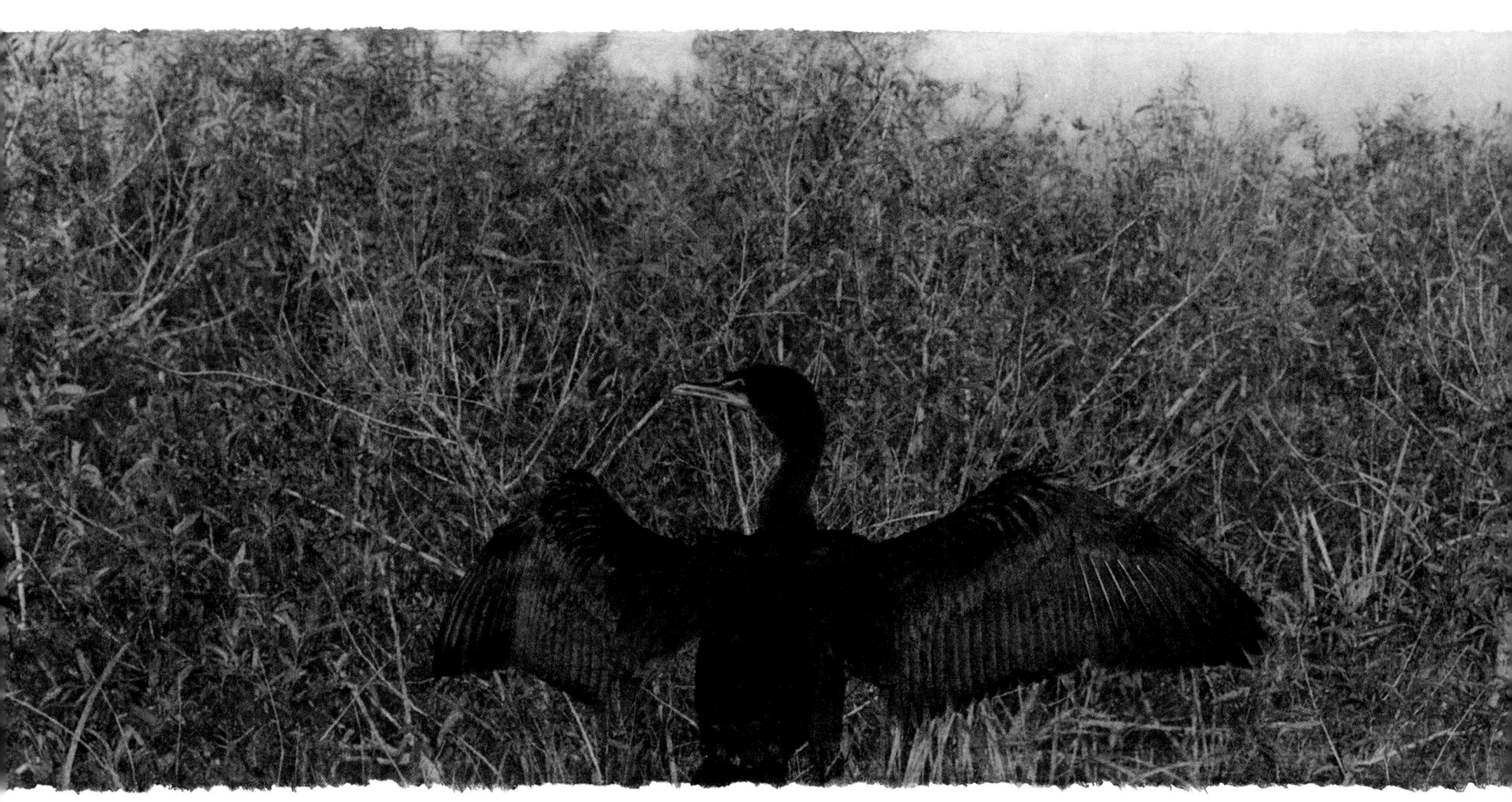

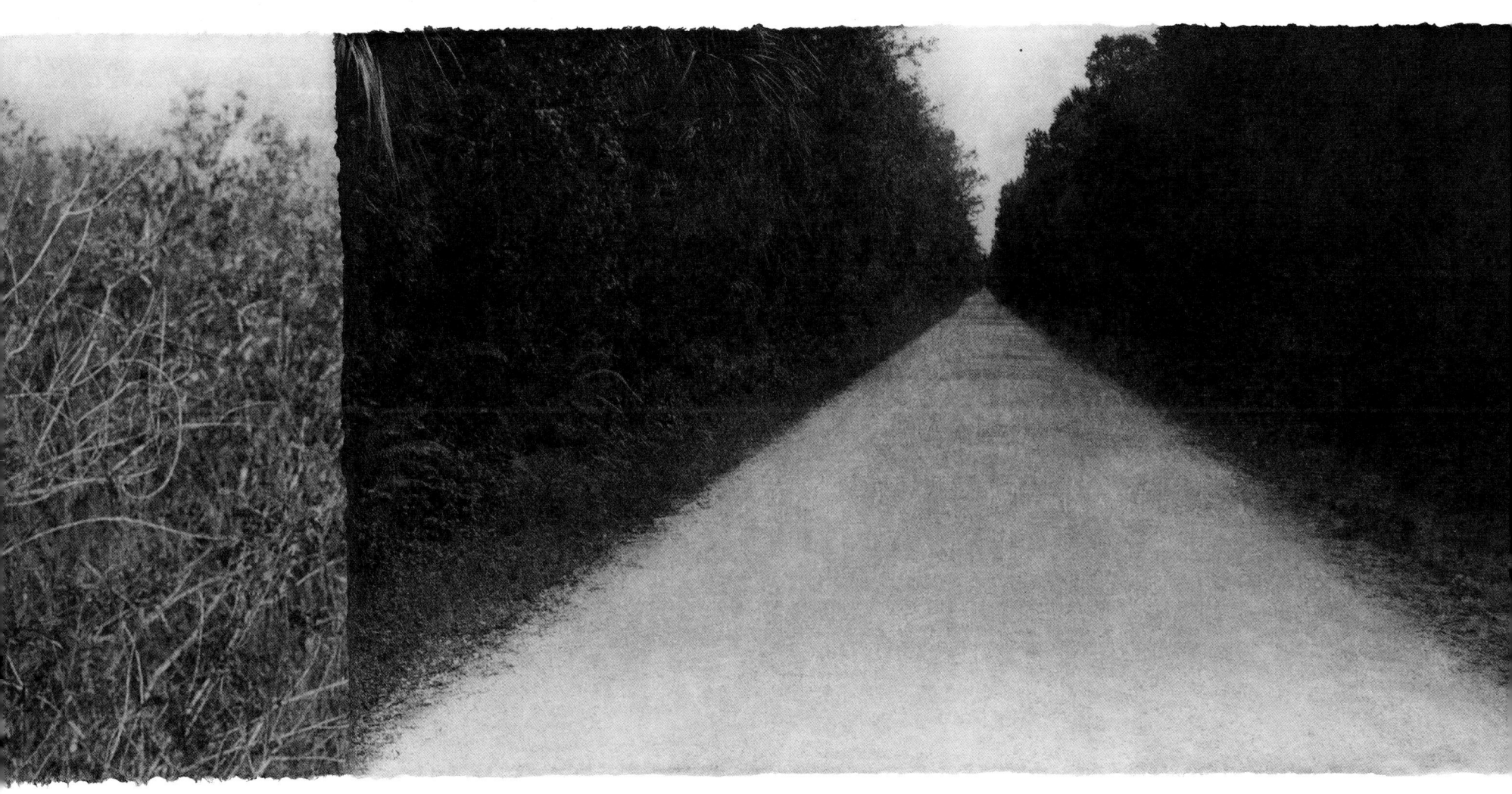

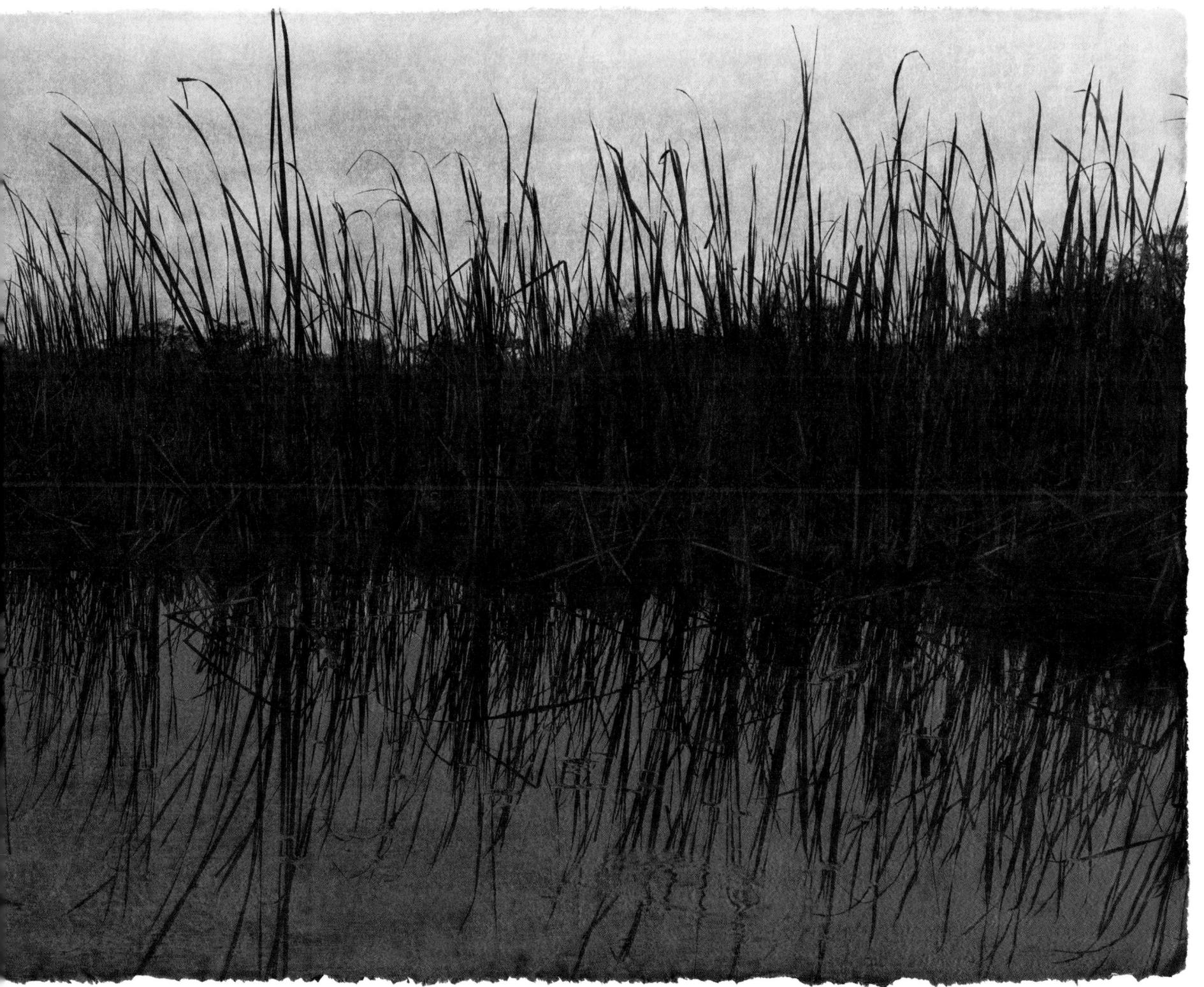

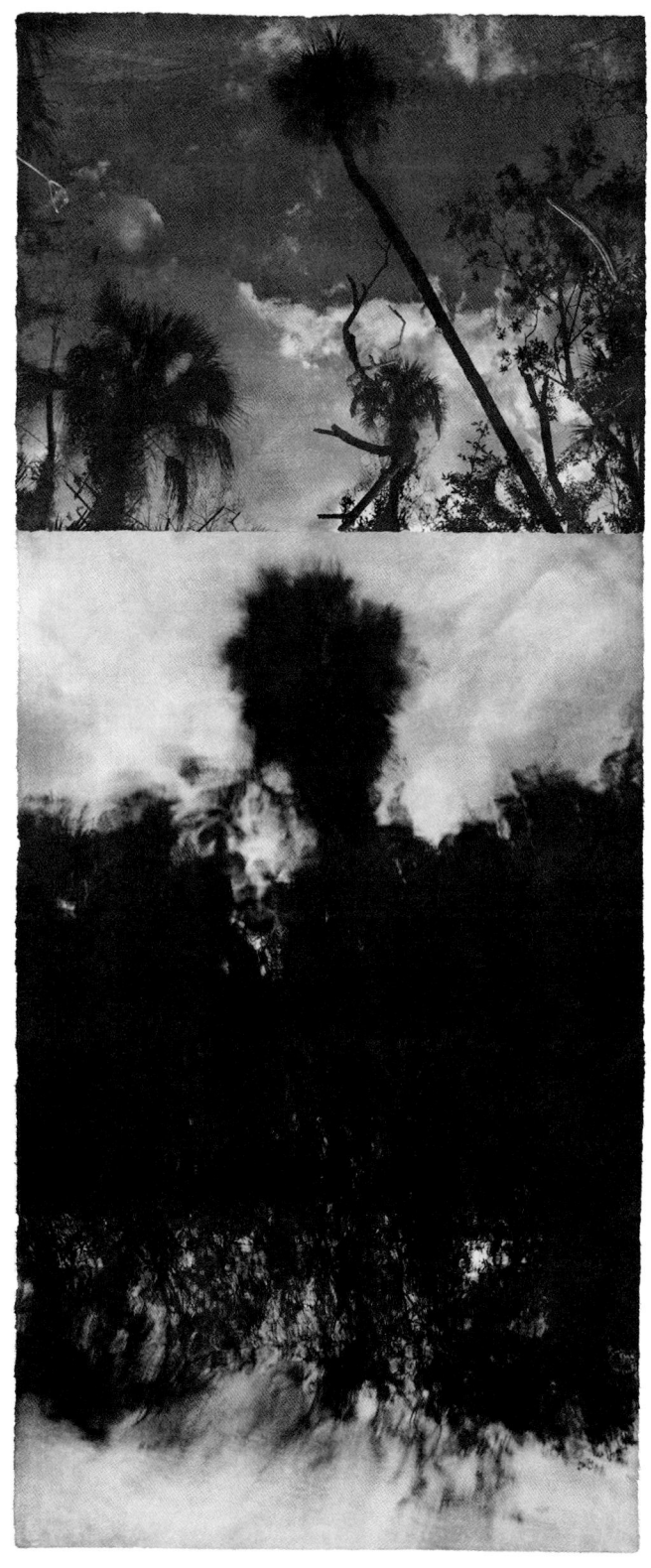

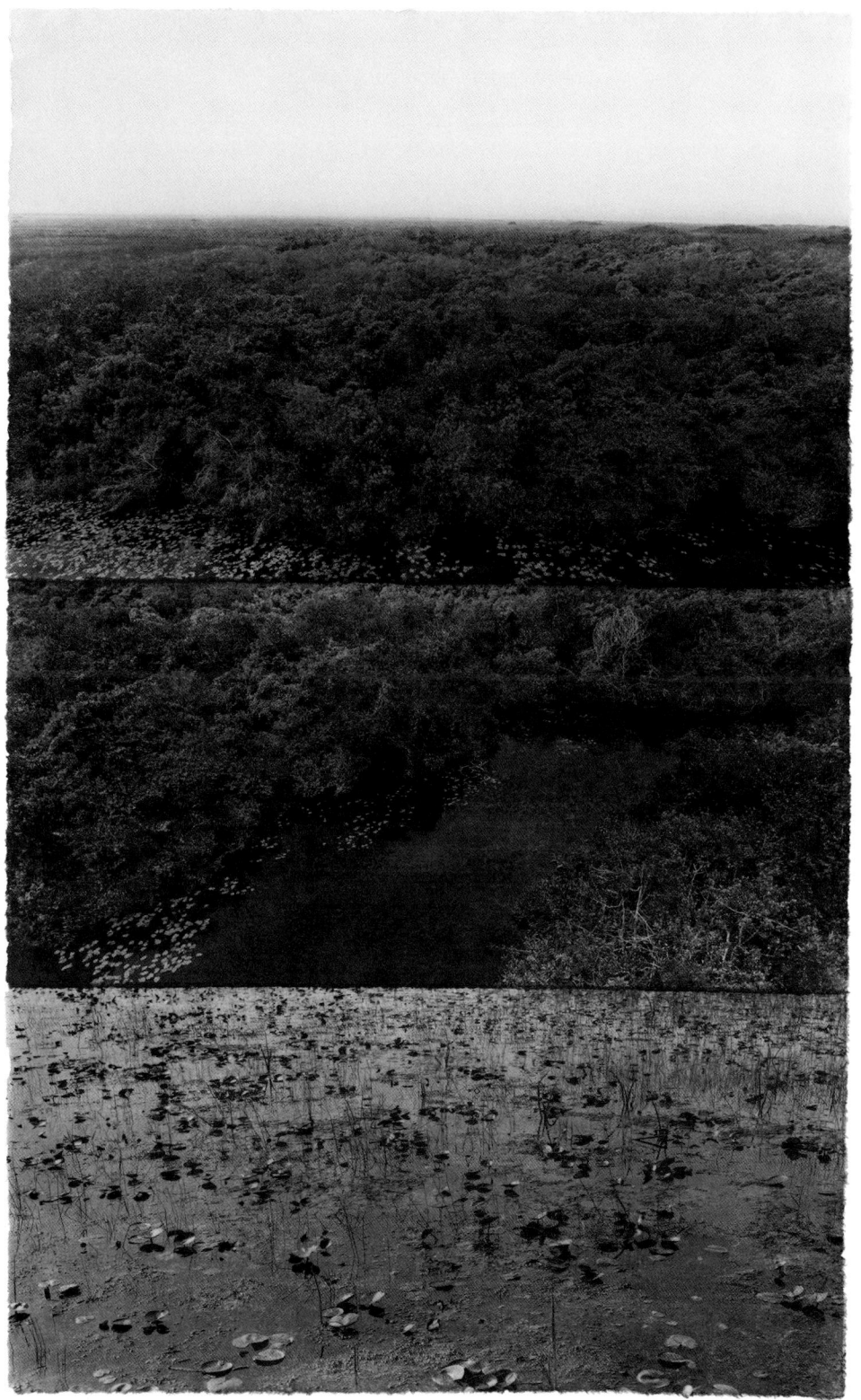

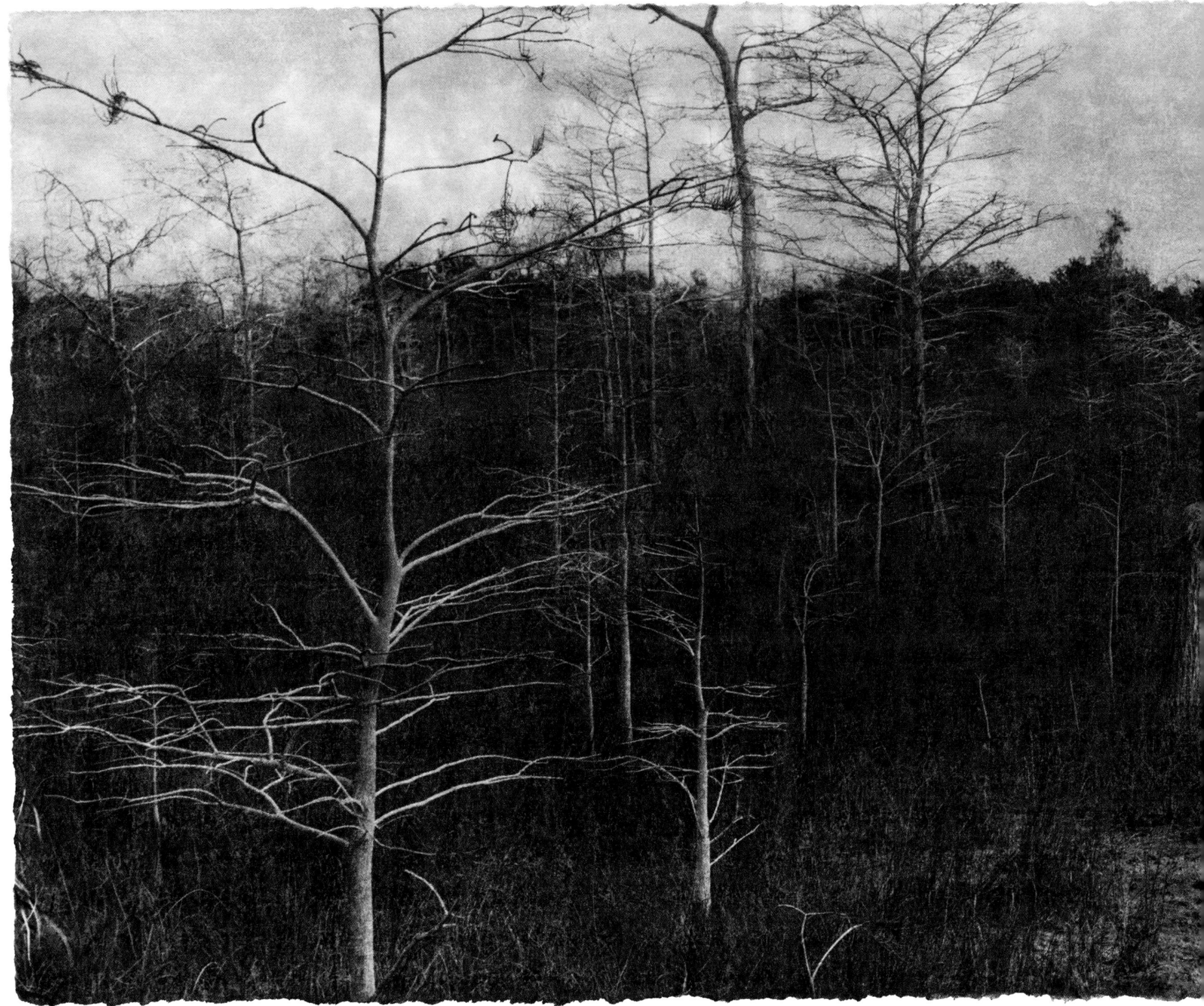

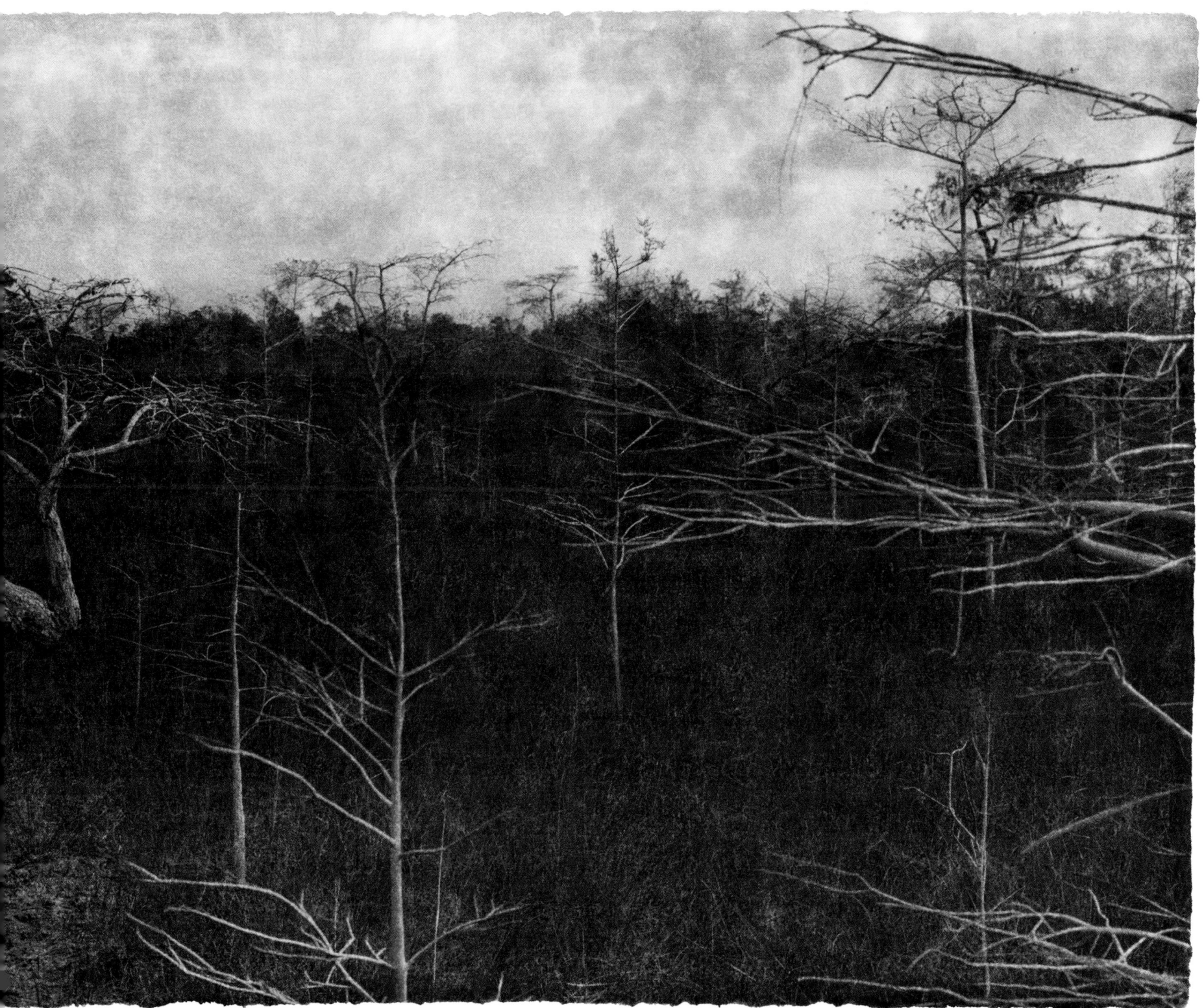

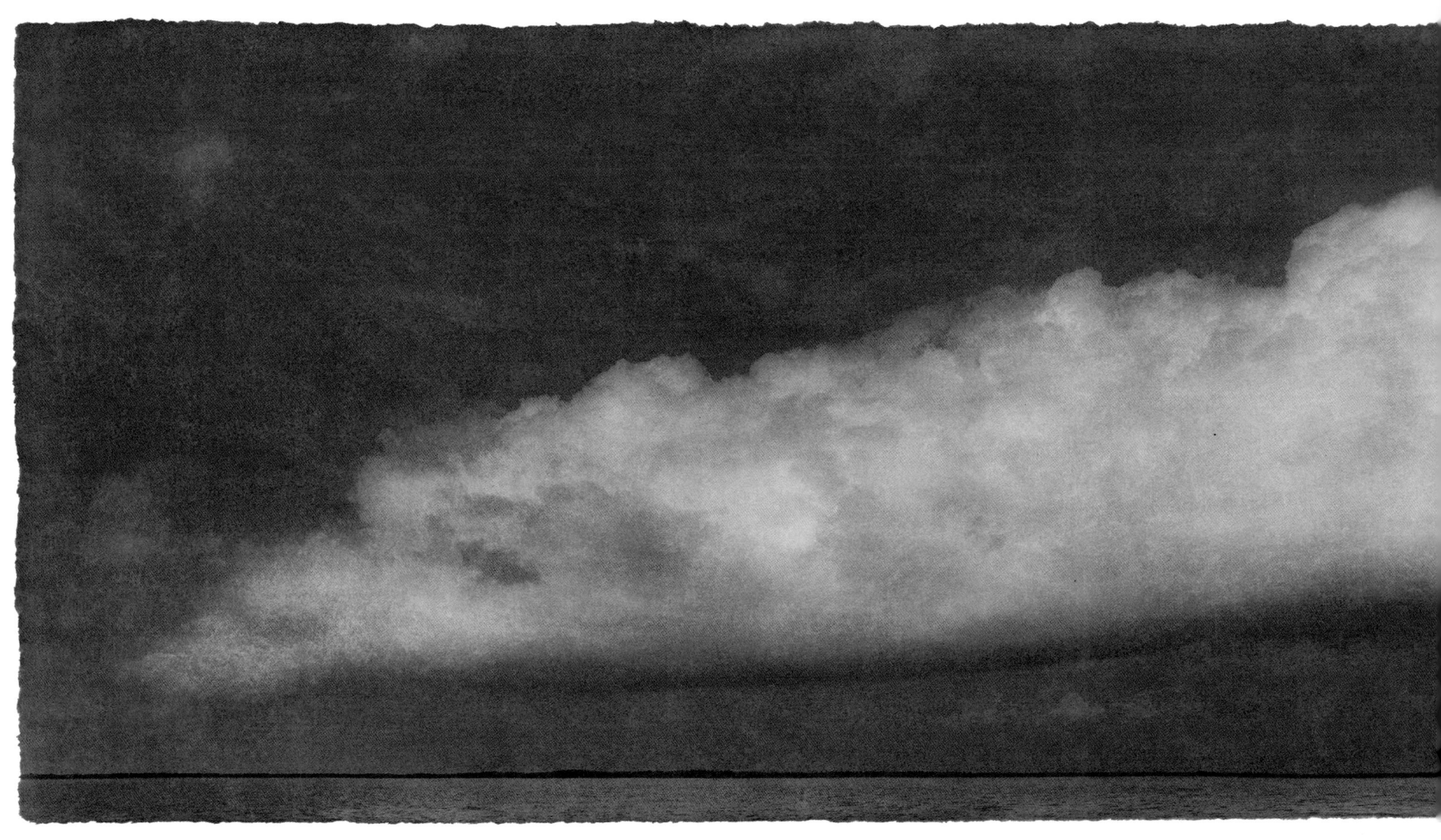

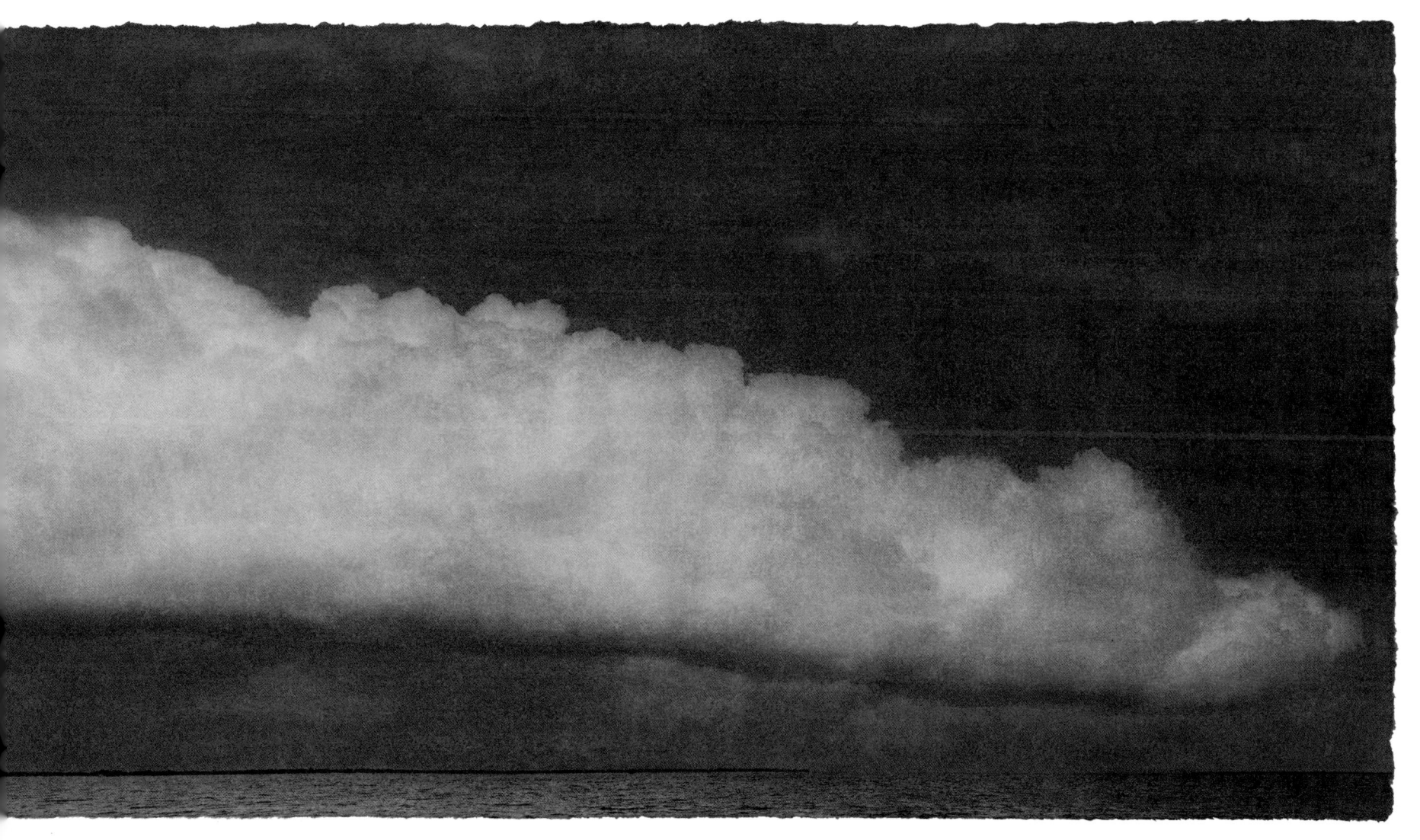

# BERT TEUNISSEN

# Bert Teunissen

BERT TEUNISSEN LIVES AND WORKS ACROSS THE
HARBOR FROM THE CENTER OF AMSTERDAM. FOR
MORE THAN TWO DECADES HE HAS BEEN MAKING
PORTRAITS OF EUROPEANS POSED IN THEIR
DOMESTIC SPACES. HE VIEWS HIS WORK AS BOTH
AN ANTHROPOLOGICAL STUDY AND A STUDY OF
NATIONAL CHARACTER. CARRYING THIS STRATEGY
INTO THE EVERGLADES, TEUNISSEN HAS MADE IMAGES
OF PEOPLE IN THEIR DOMESTIC ENVIRONMENTS,
FROM OKEECHOBEE TO EVERGLADES CITY. AT THE
SAME TIME, HE HAS MADE A VISUAL RECORD OF HIS
JOURNEYS IN SOUTH FLORIDA AND THE IMPRESSIONS
HE COULD RECORD FROM HIS RENTED CAR. THE
RESULTING GRIDS OF IMAGES CONVEY AN EXPERIENCE
OF BOTH DIARISTIC AND ANTHROPOLOGICAL
SIGNIFICANCE.

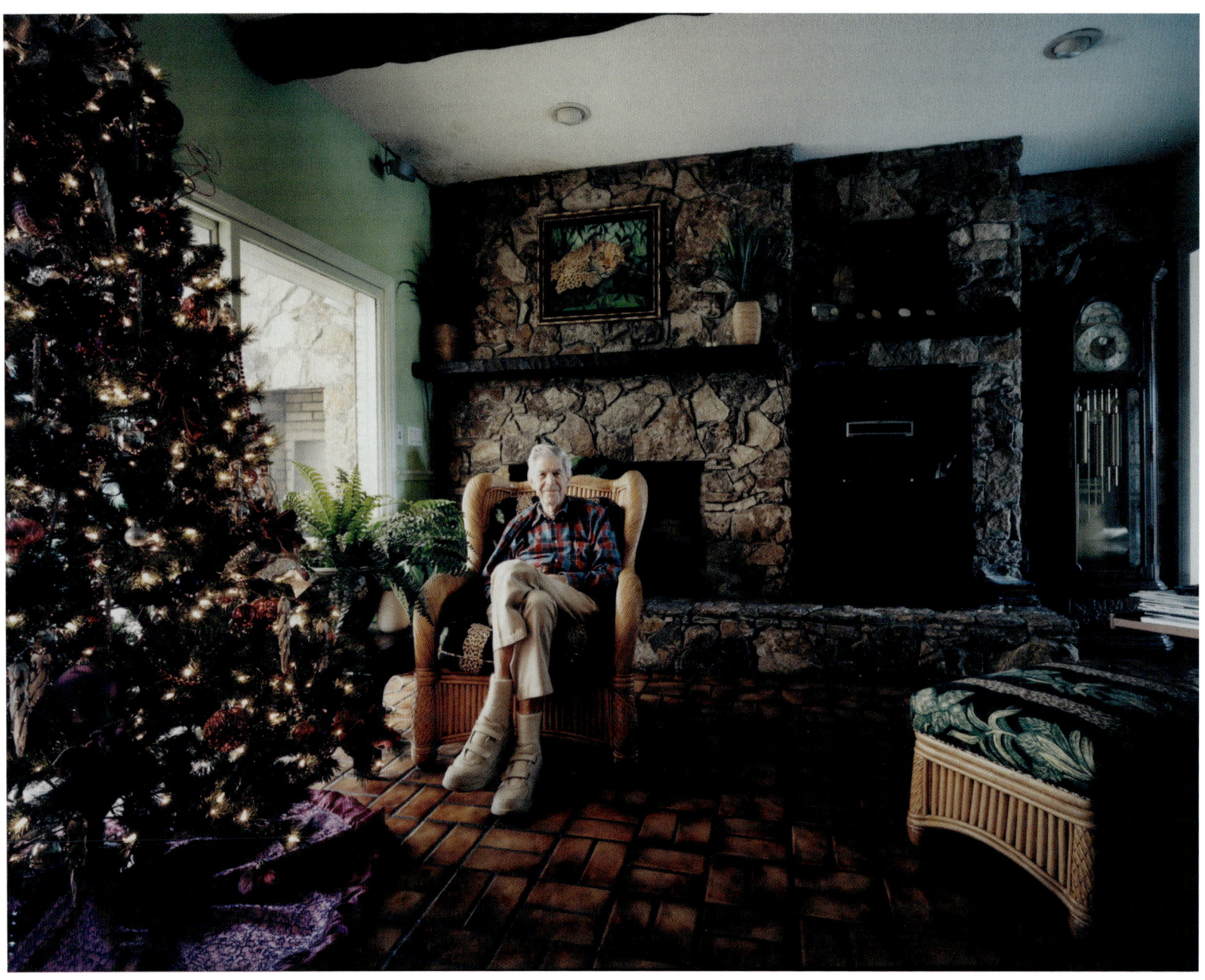

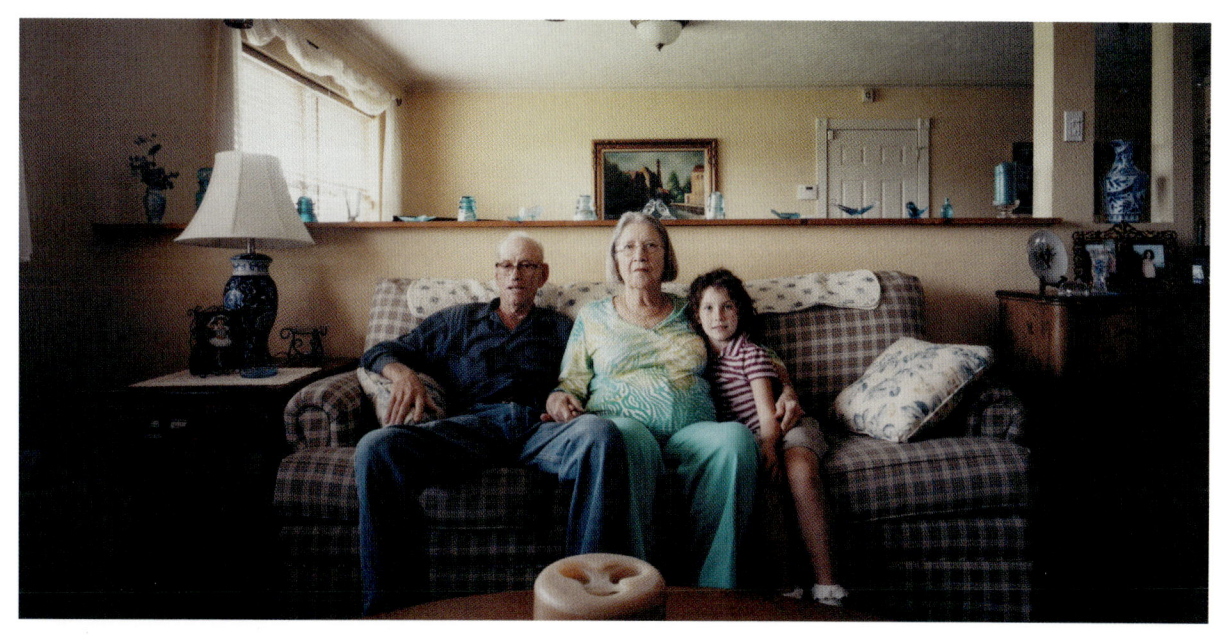

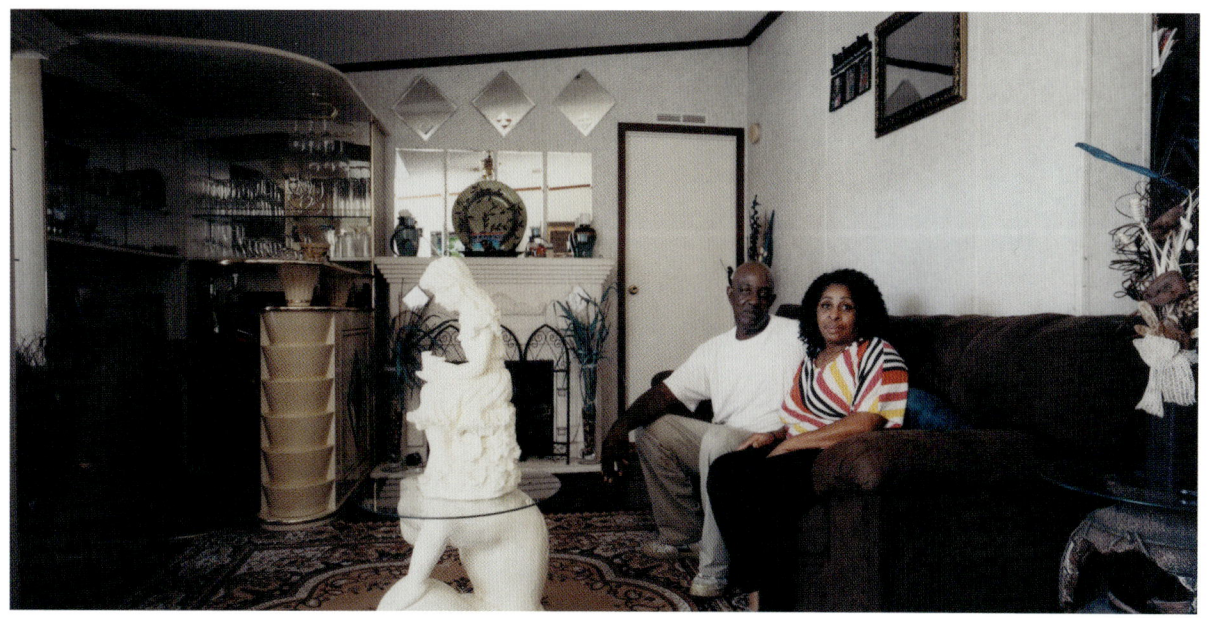

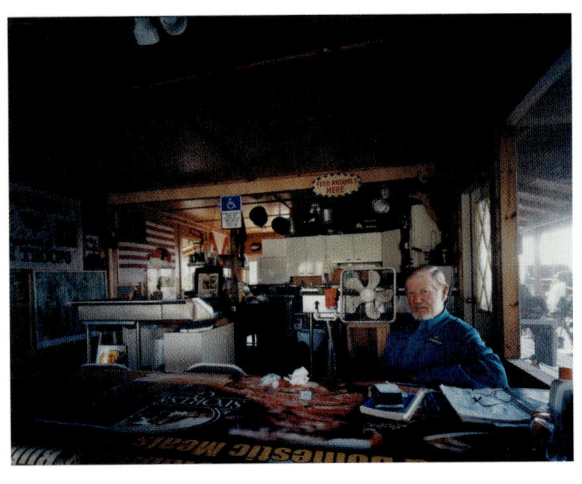
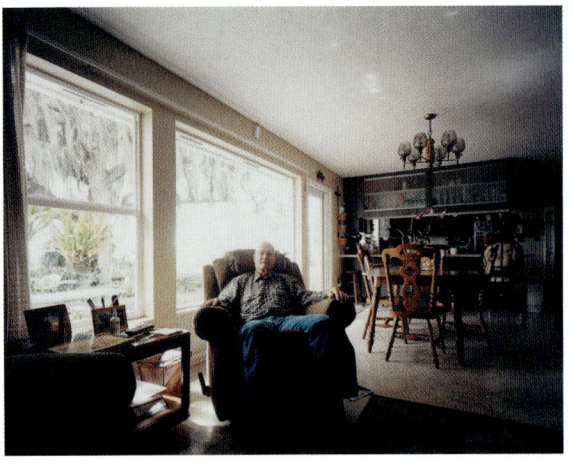
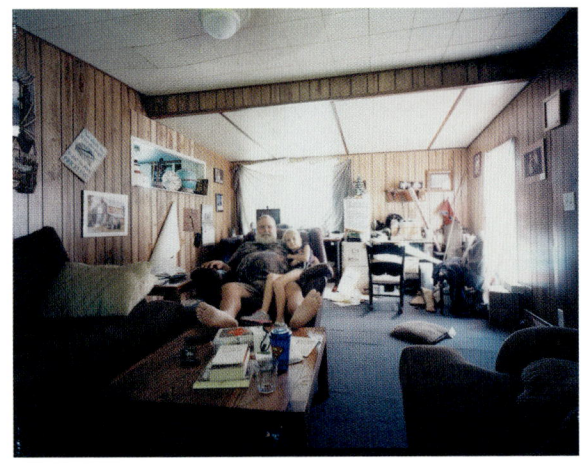
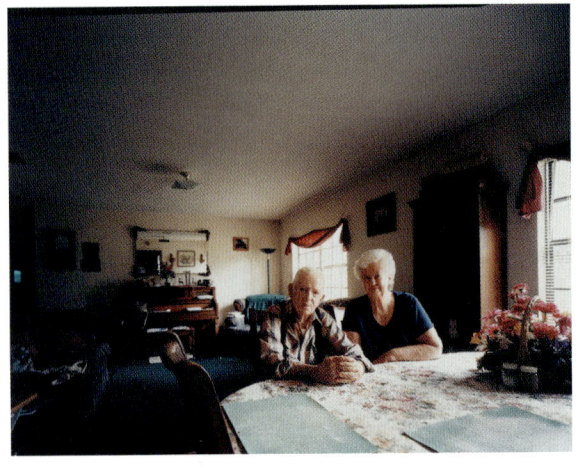
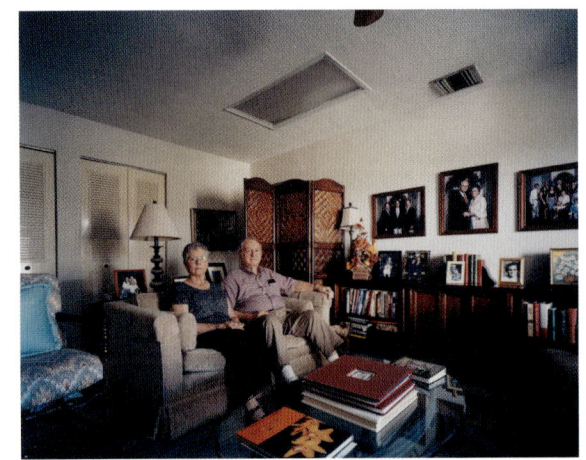
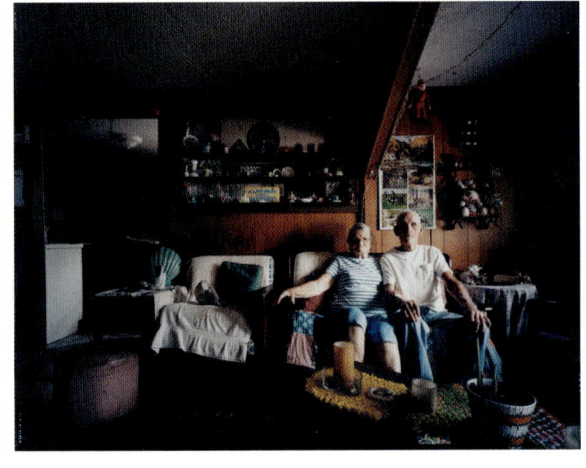
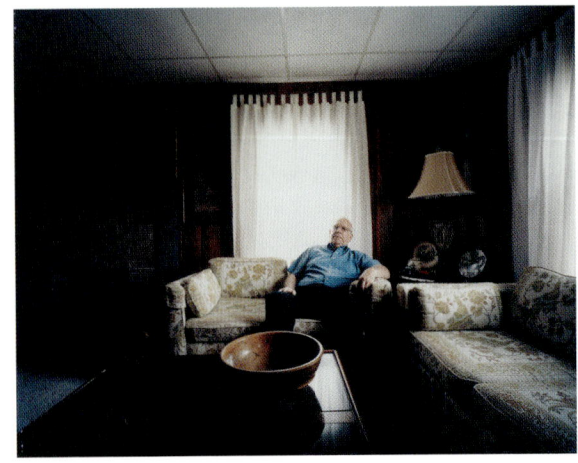
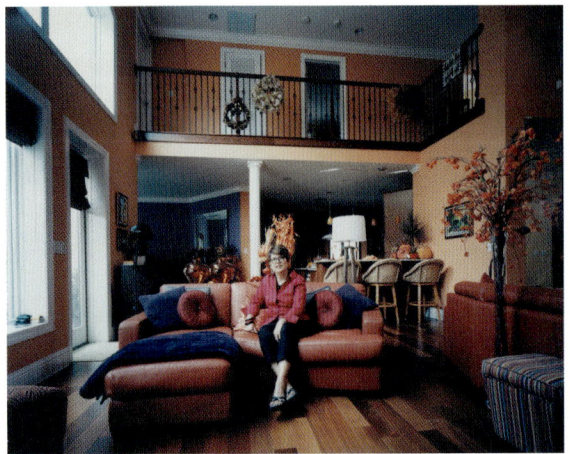
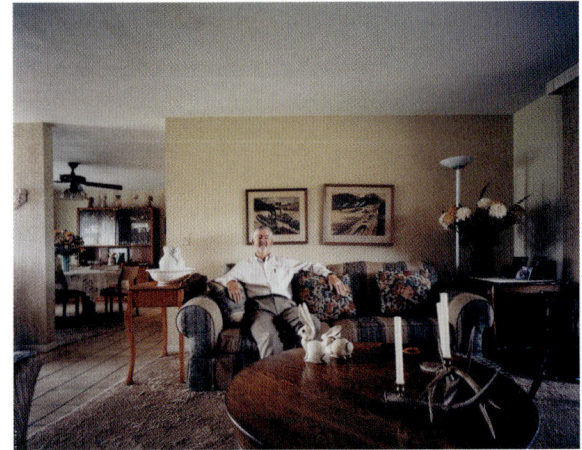

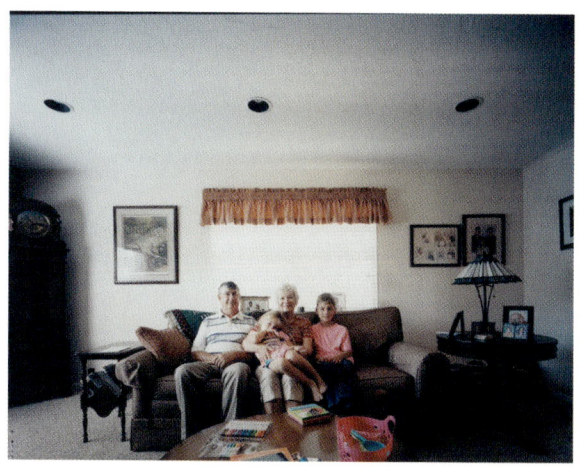
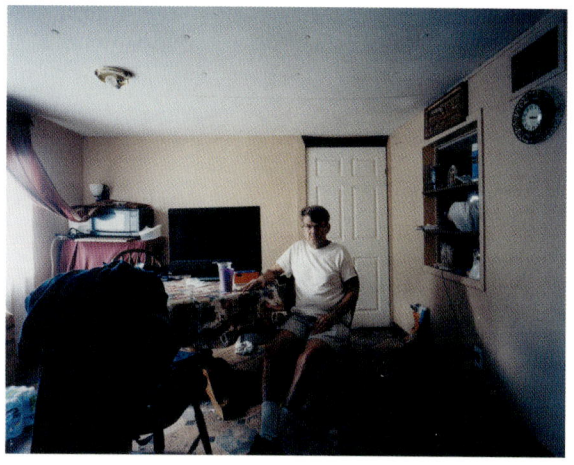
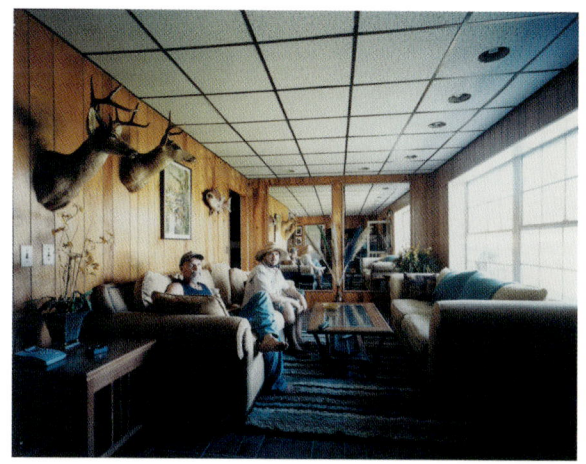
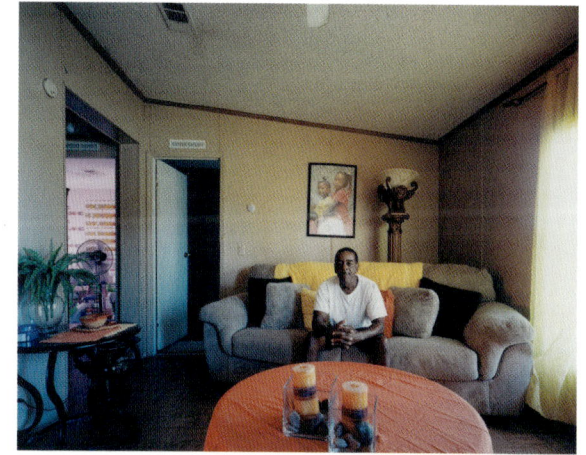
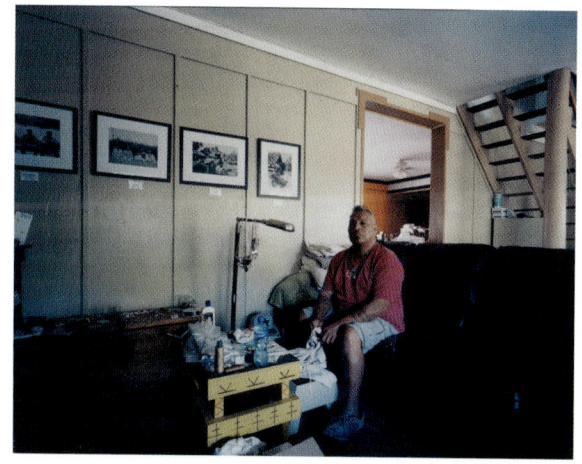
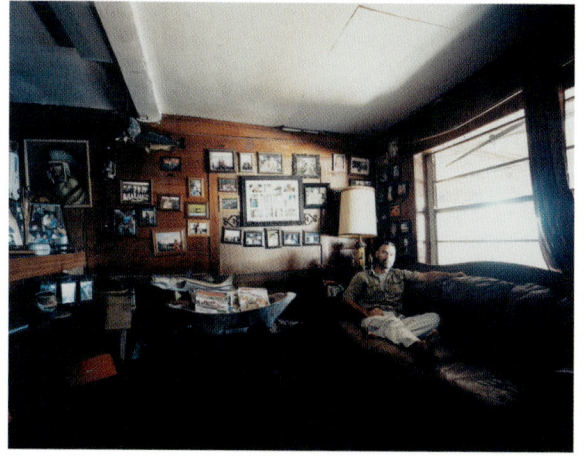
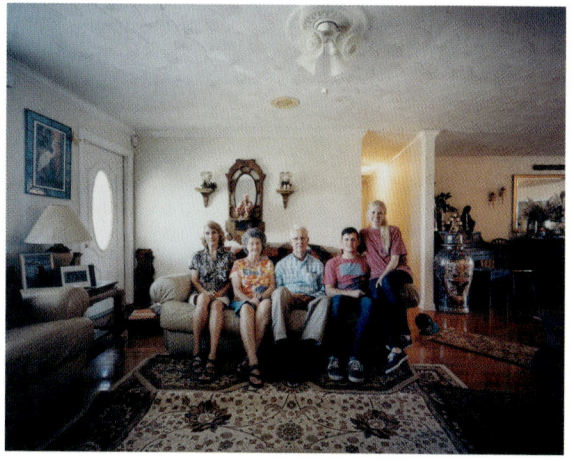
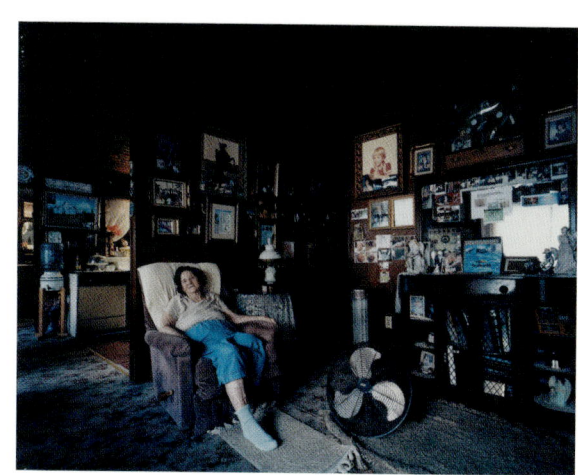

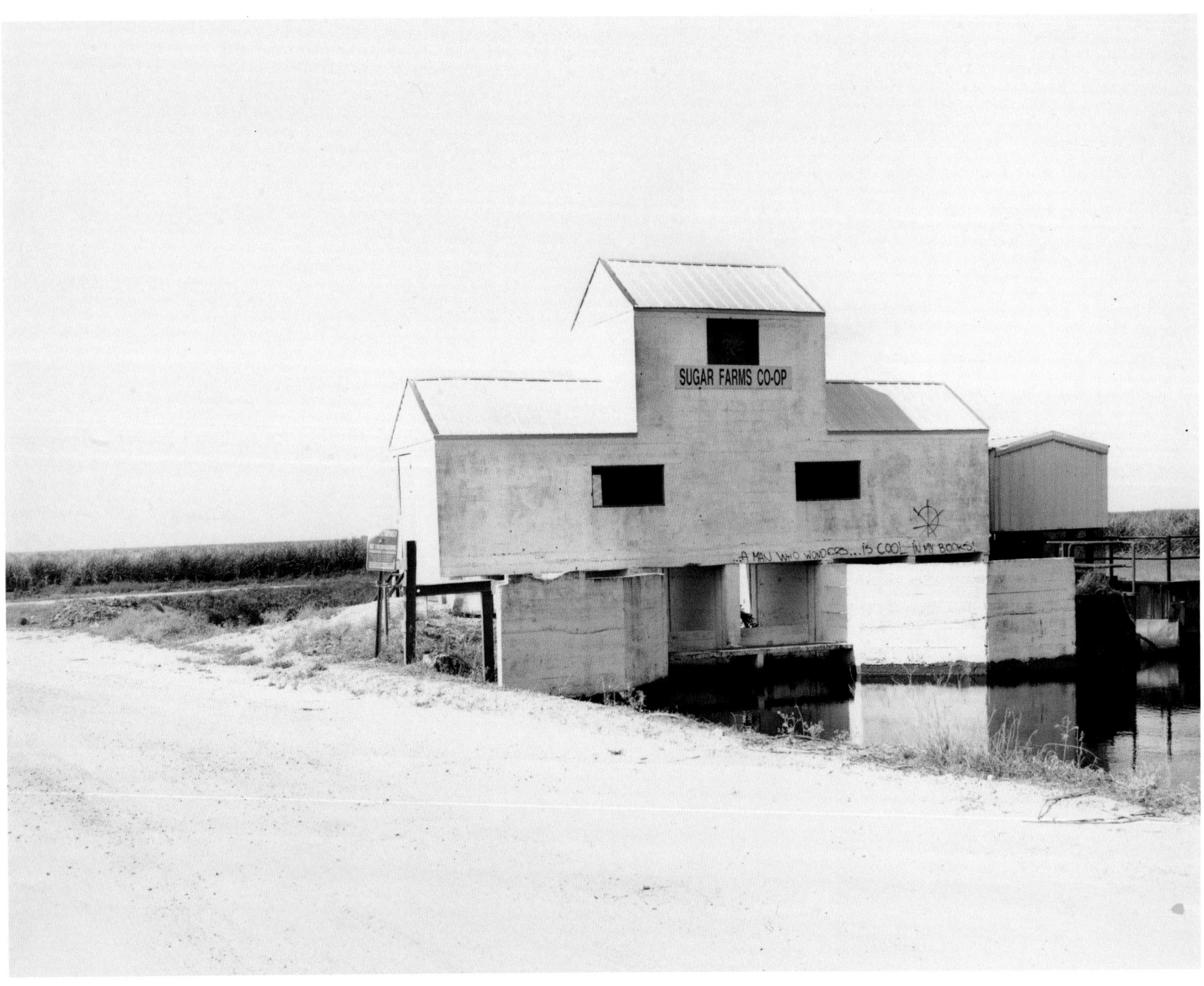

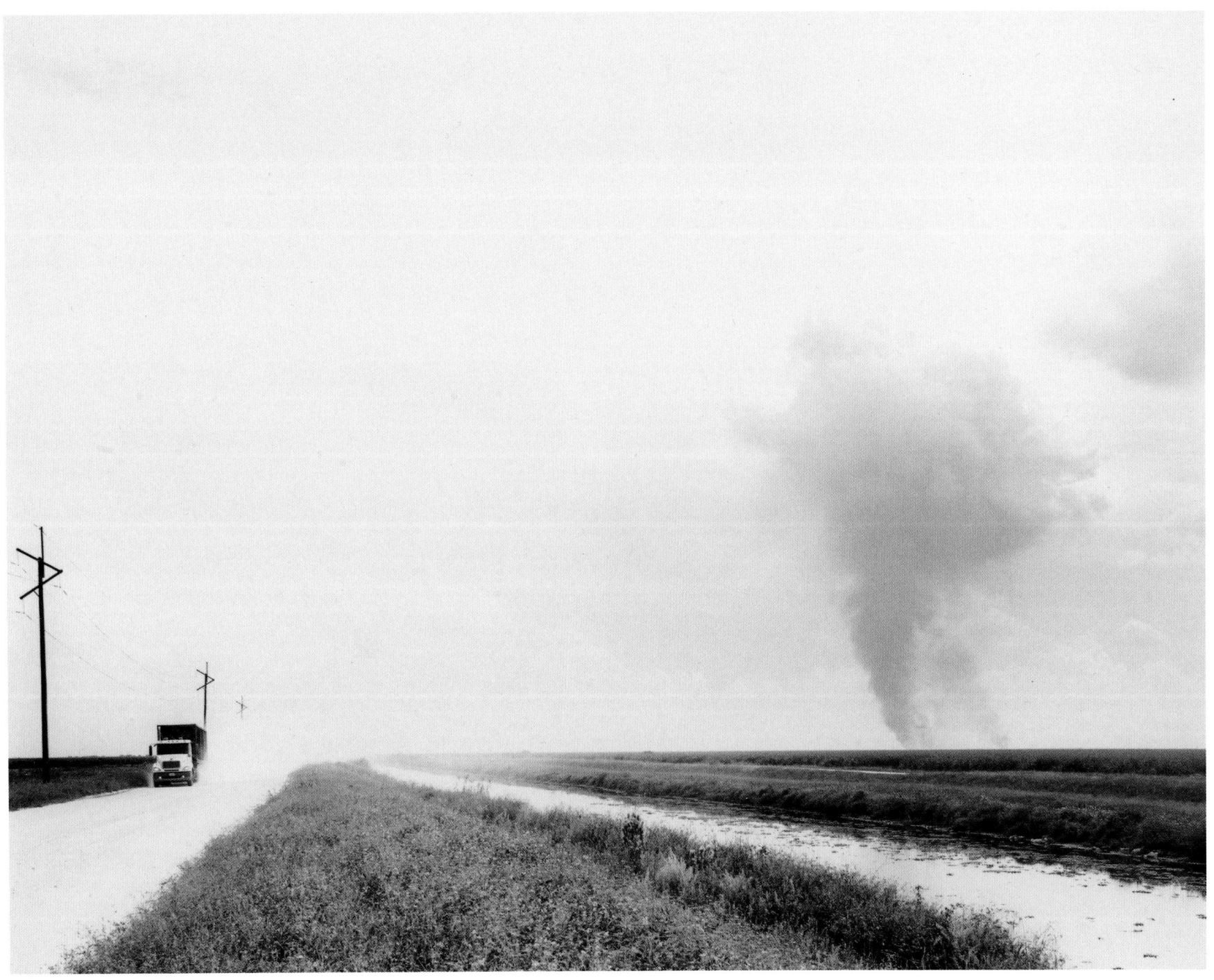

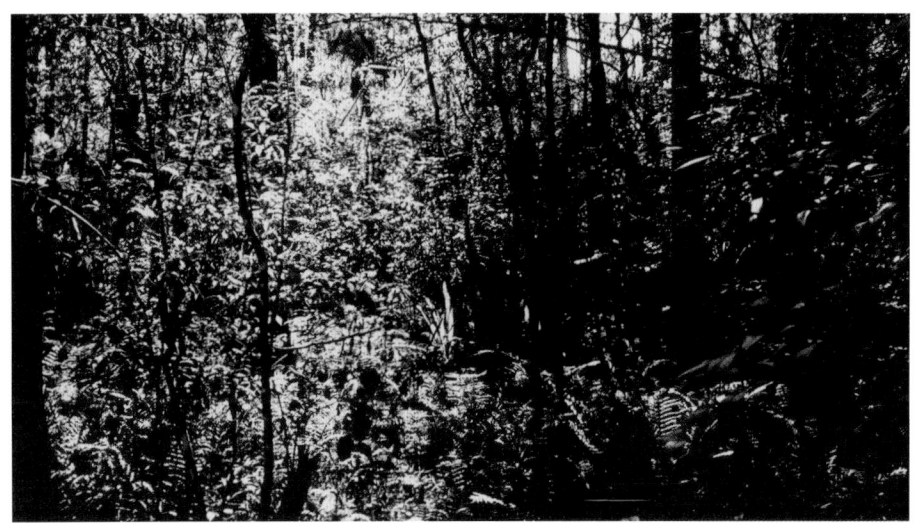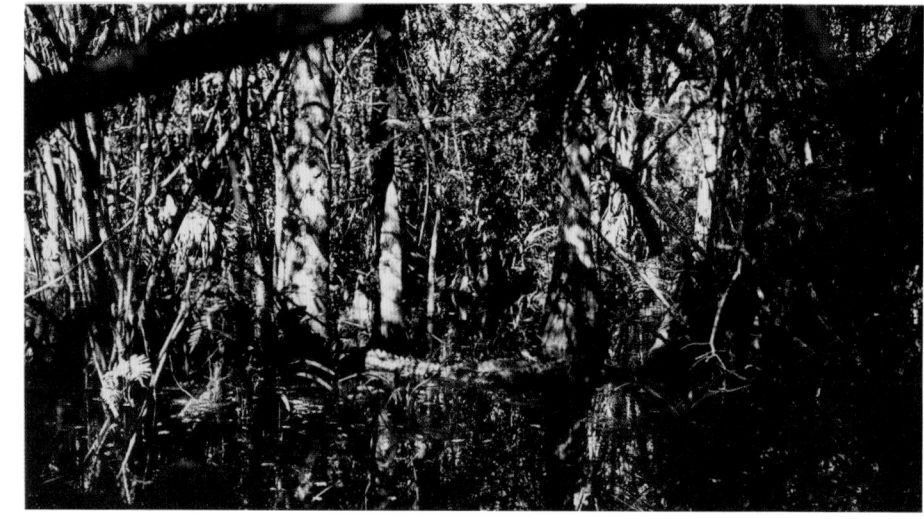

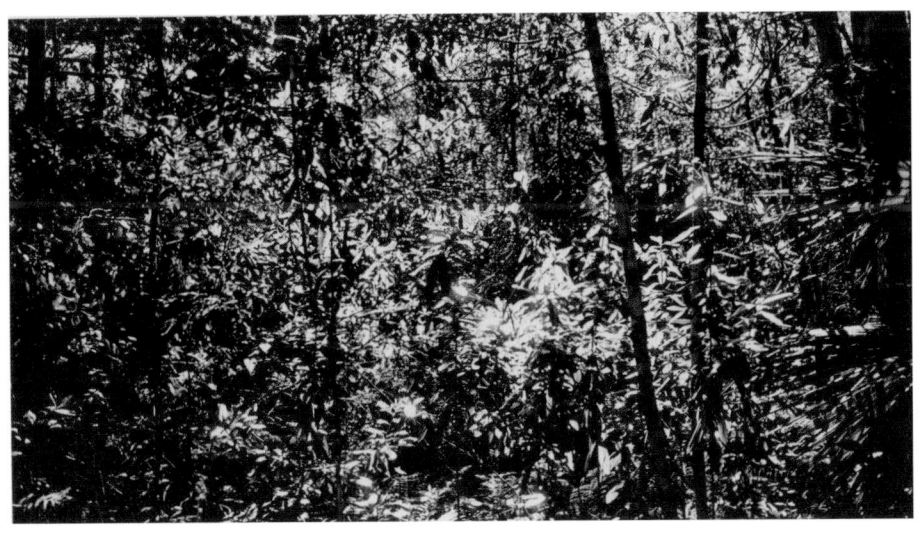 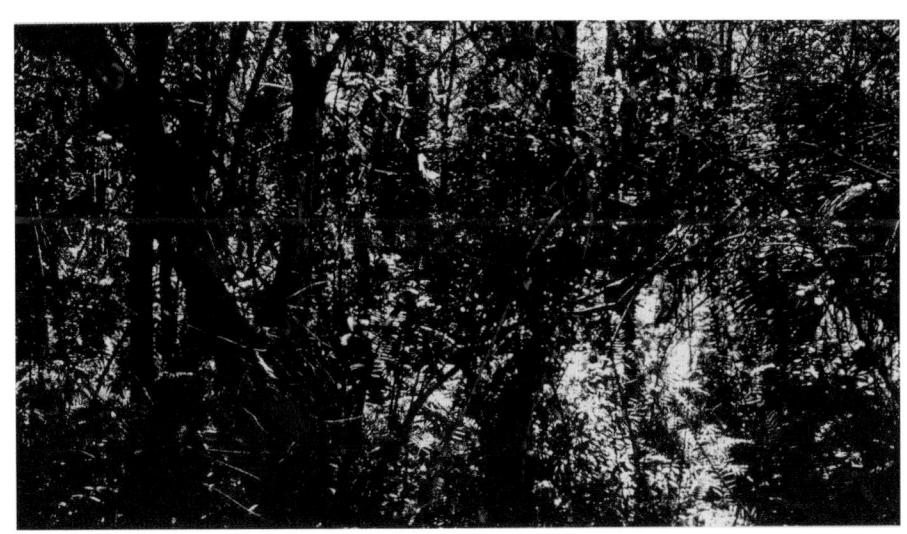

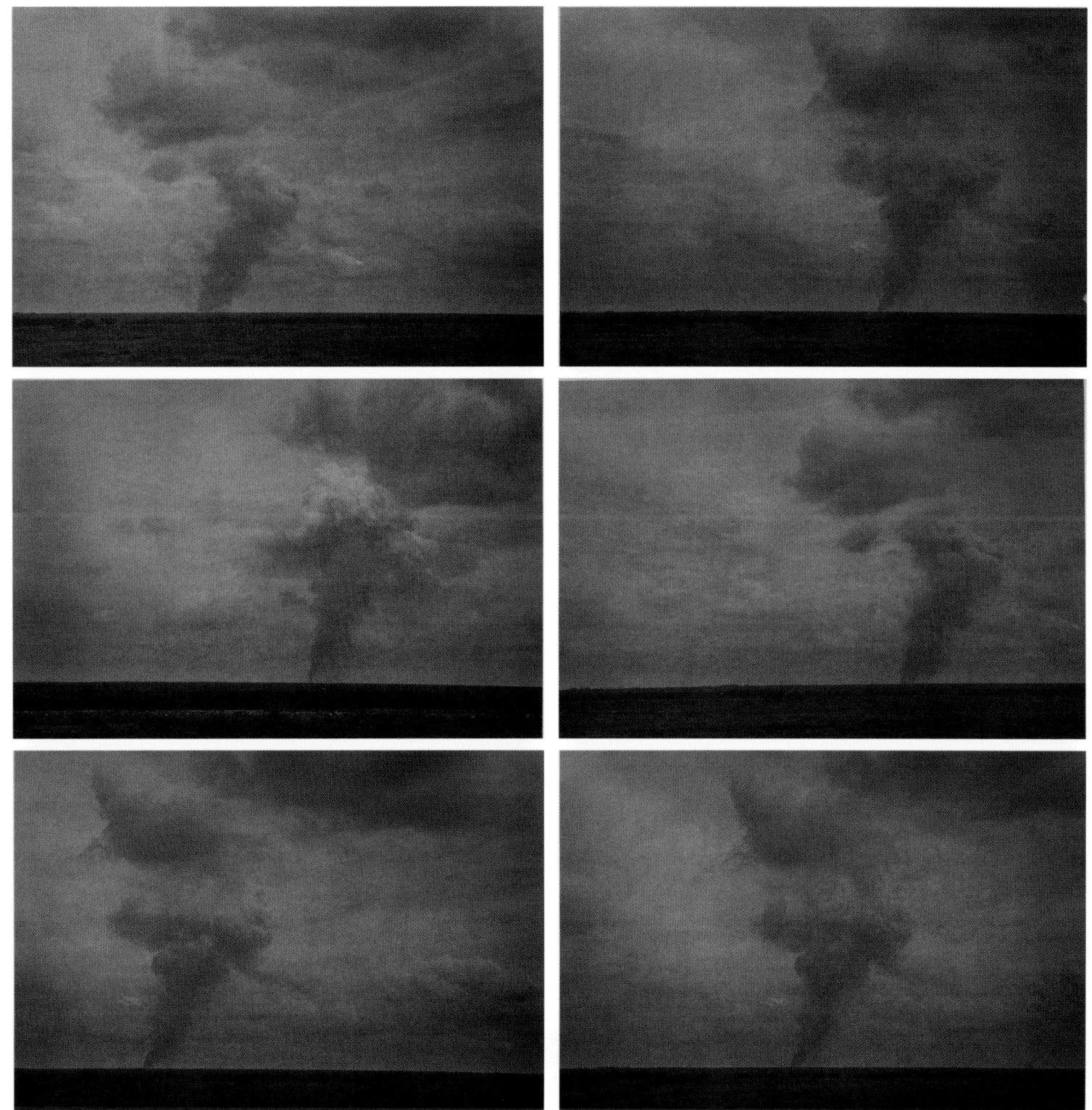

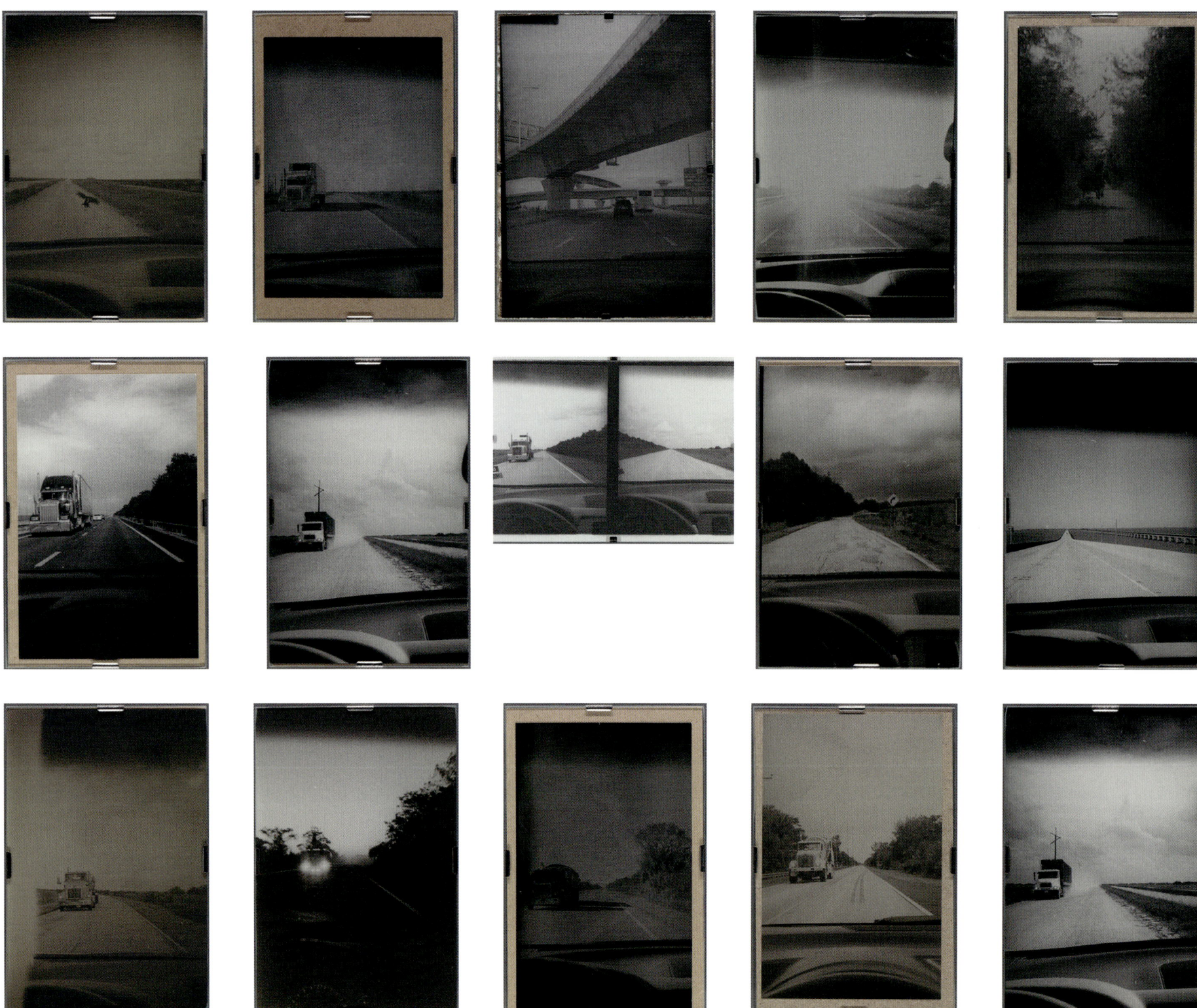

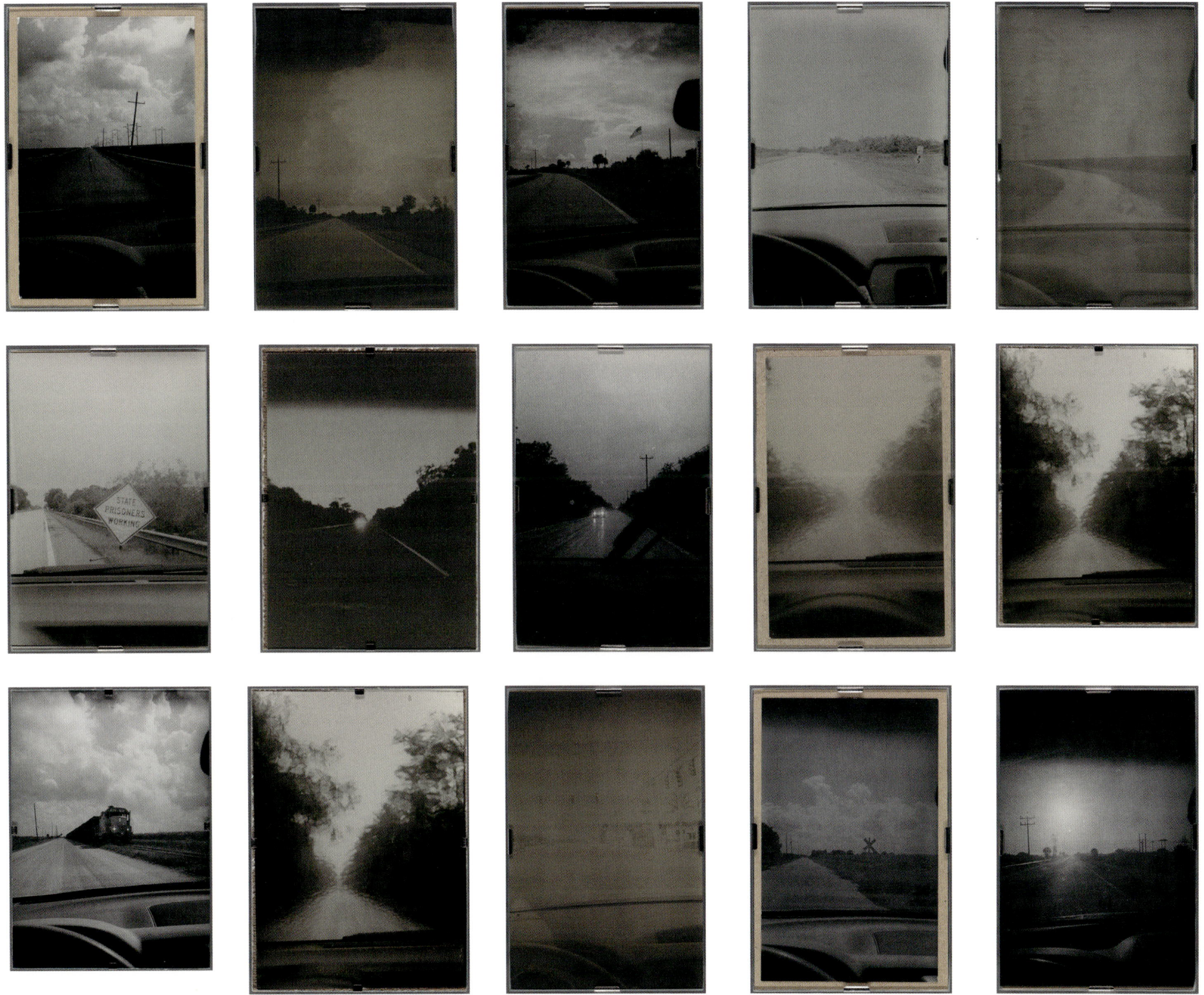

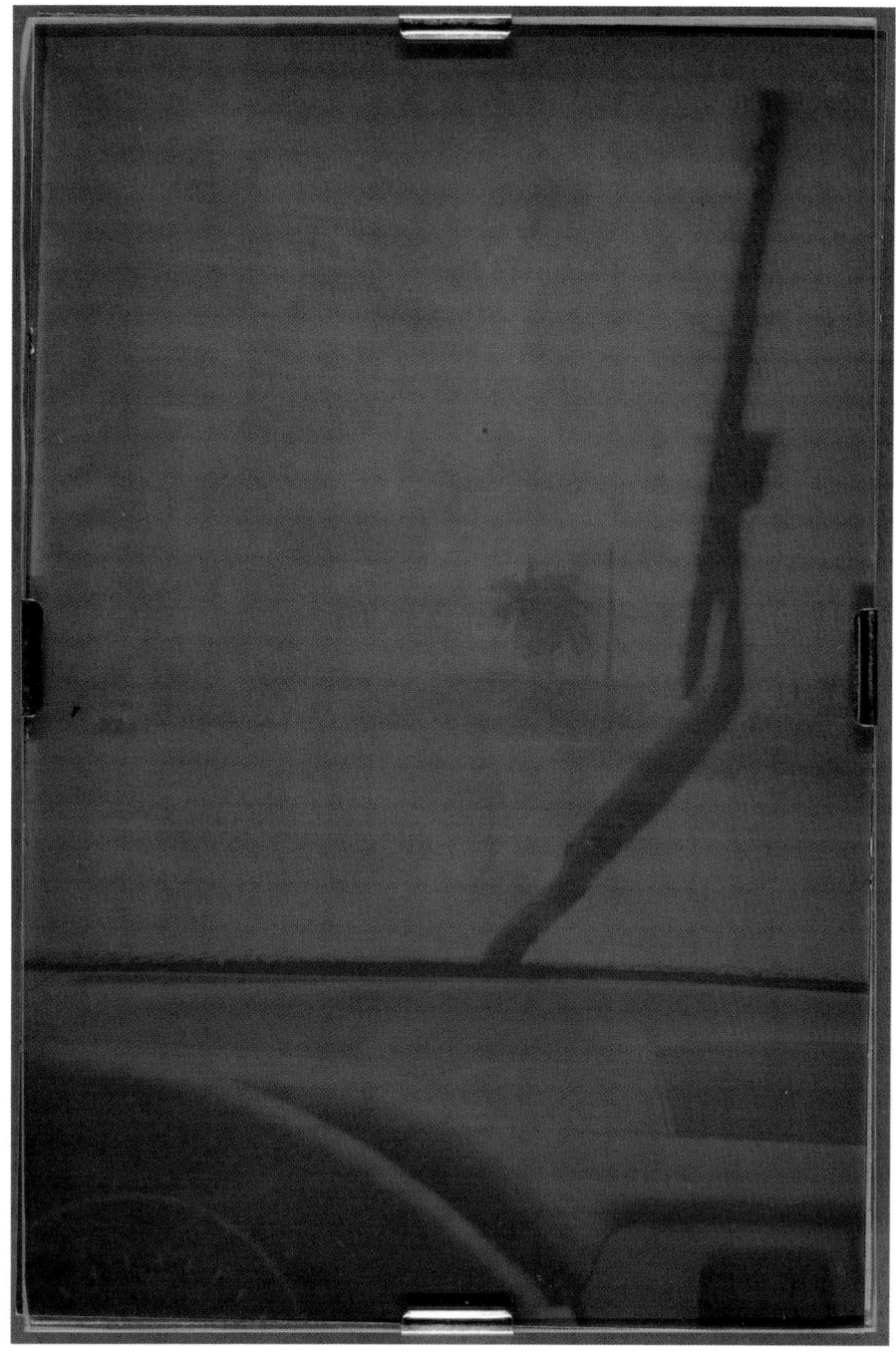

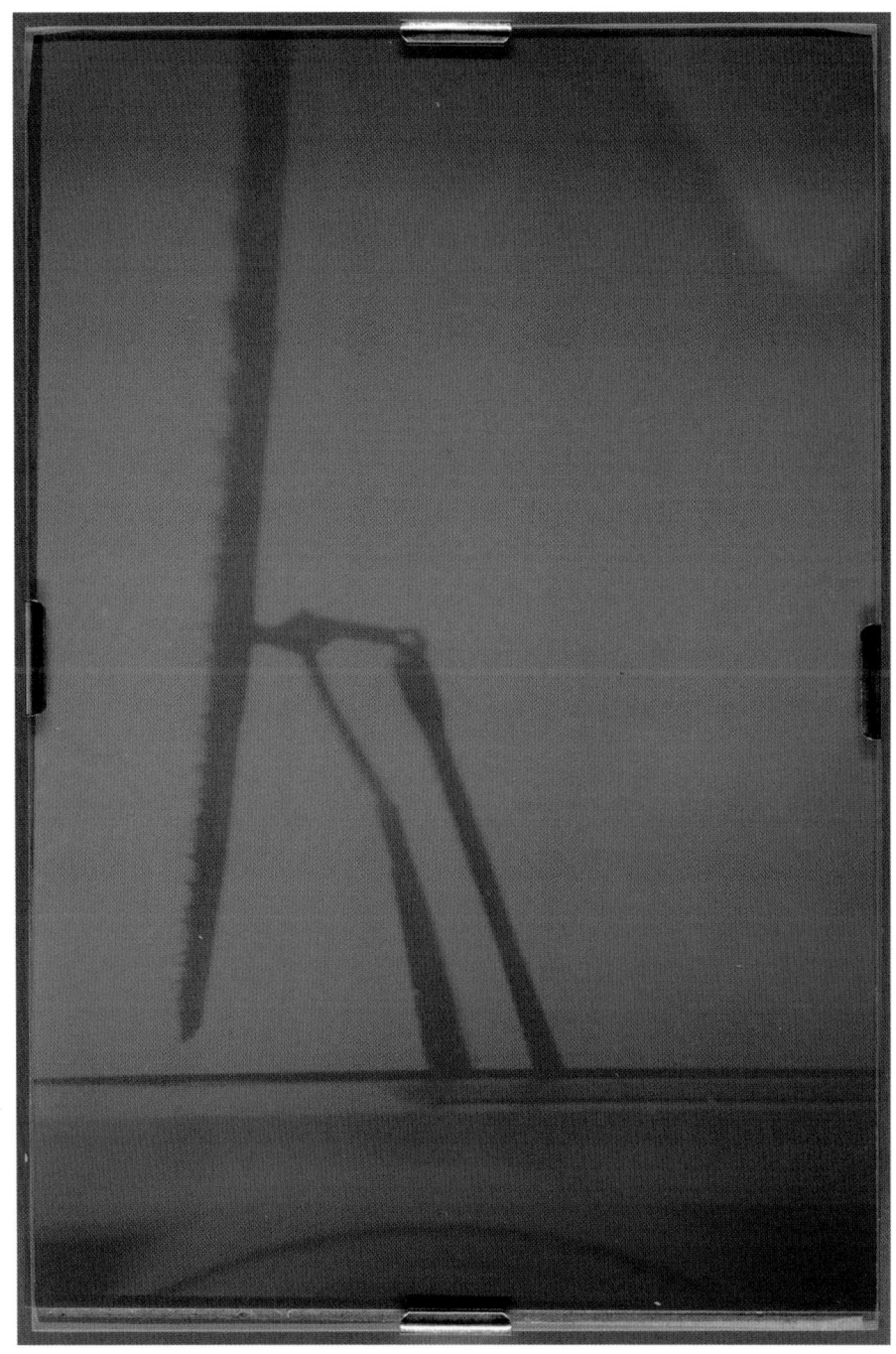

GERALD
SLOTA

# Gerald Slota

NEW JERSEY–BASED GERALD SLOTA HAS BEEN
WORKING WITH AND ALSO WORKING UPON IMAGES
FOR HIS ENTIRE CAREER. HIS WORKING METHOD IS
HIGHLY INTUITIVE, AND HIS IMAGERY IS ACHIEVED
THROUGH A COMPLEX ACCUMULATION OF
PHOTOGRAPHY, COLLAGE, DRAWING, AND PAINTING.
HIS COMPOSITIONS EXHIBIT A VIOLENT TEARING
AND PIERCING ALONGSIDE A SENSITIVE, EVEN
TENDER RENDERING OF COLOR AND TONE. SLOTA HAS
LONG BEEN INTRIGUED WITH THE STRATEGIES AND
FORMATS OF EARLY RENAISSANCE AS WELL AS 17TH-
AND 18TH-CENTURY HISTORY PAINTINGS. PAIRING
THIS INTEREST WITH HIS OWN IDIOSYNCRATIC
SYSTEM OF IMAGE CREATION, SLOTA HAS PRODUCED A
SINGLE, MONUMENTAL NARRATIVE PANORAMA THAT
CONJURES THE CONFLATED 19TH-CENTURY HISTORIES
OF THE SECOND AND THIRD SEMINOLE WARS THAT
WERE FOUGHT IN AN ATTEMPT TO PURGE SOUTHERN
FLORIDA OF THE NATIVE AND RUNAWAY SLAVE
POPULATIONS WHO HAD SOUGHT REFUGE THERE.

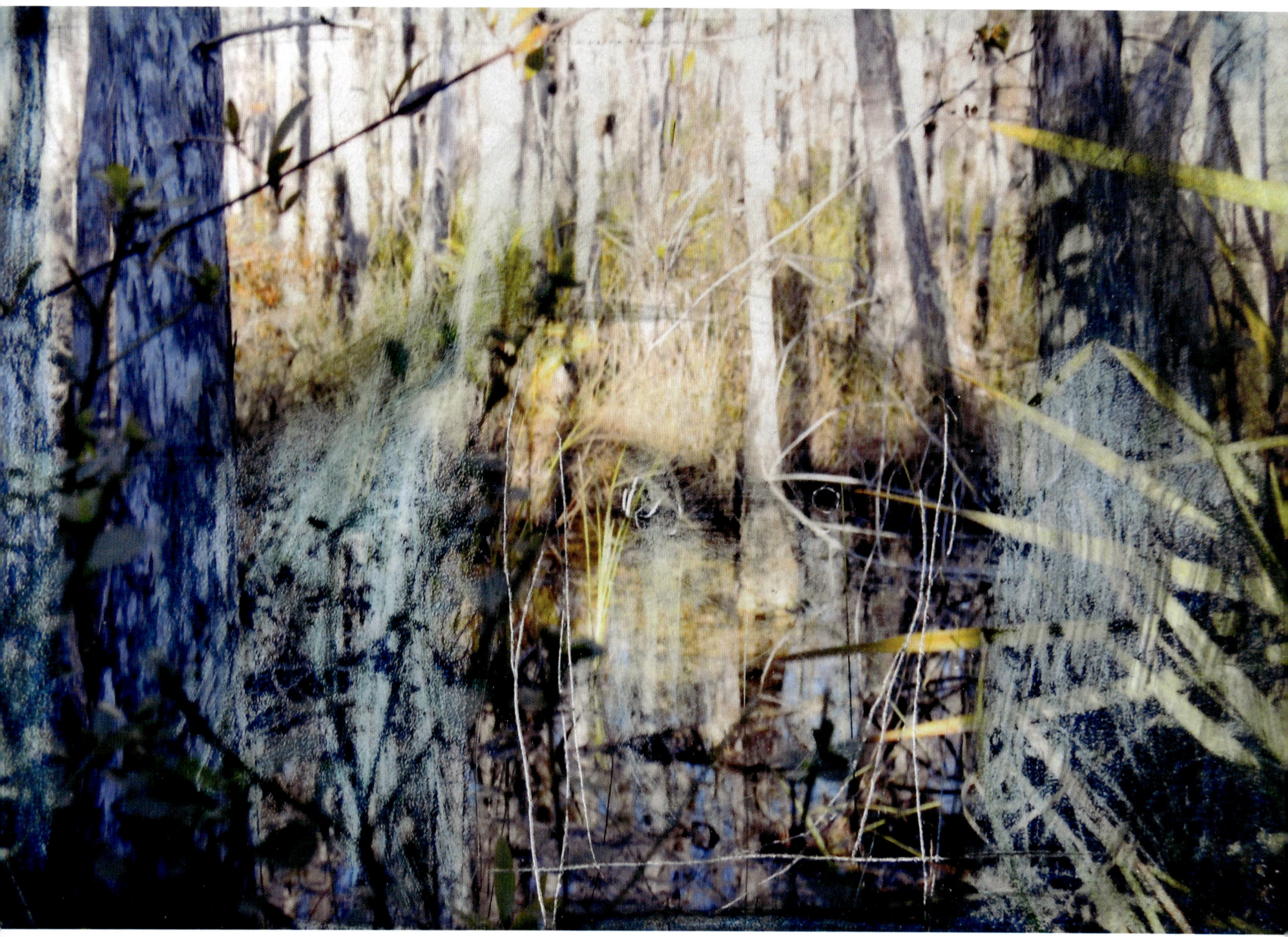

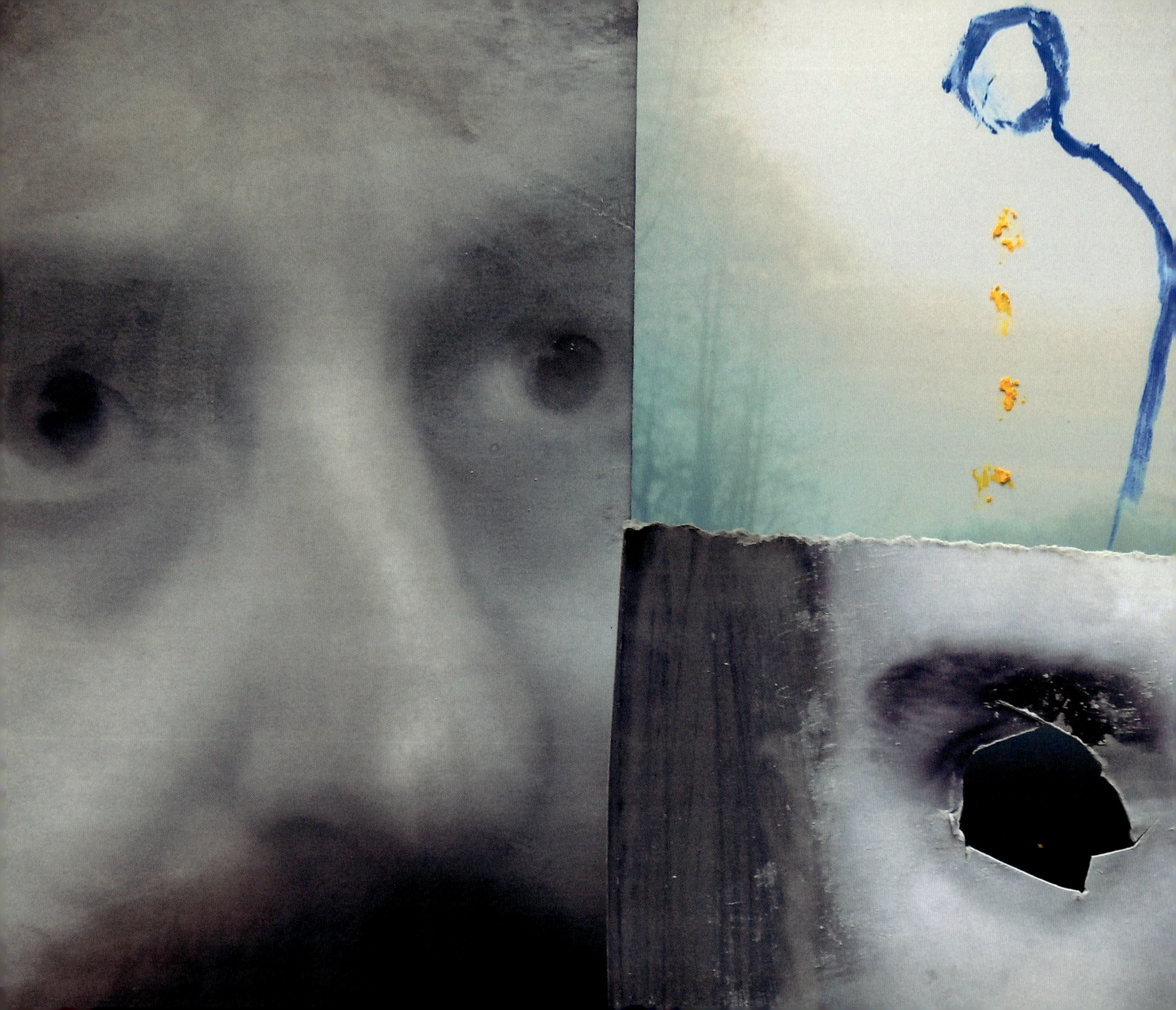

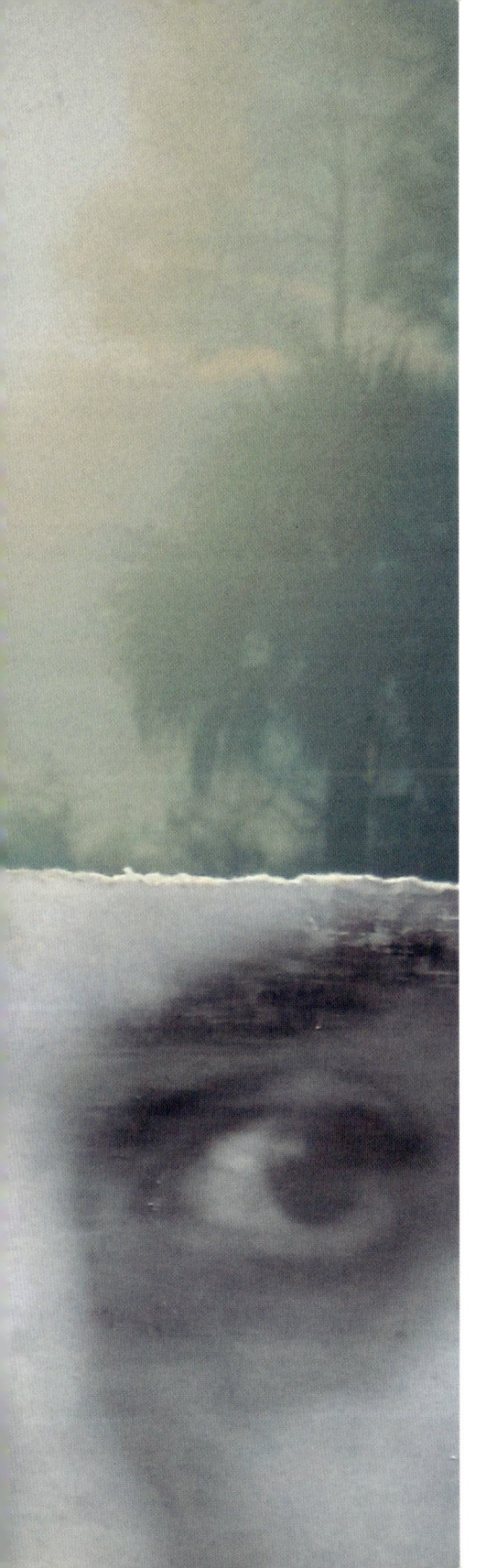

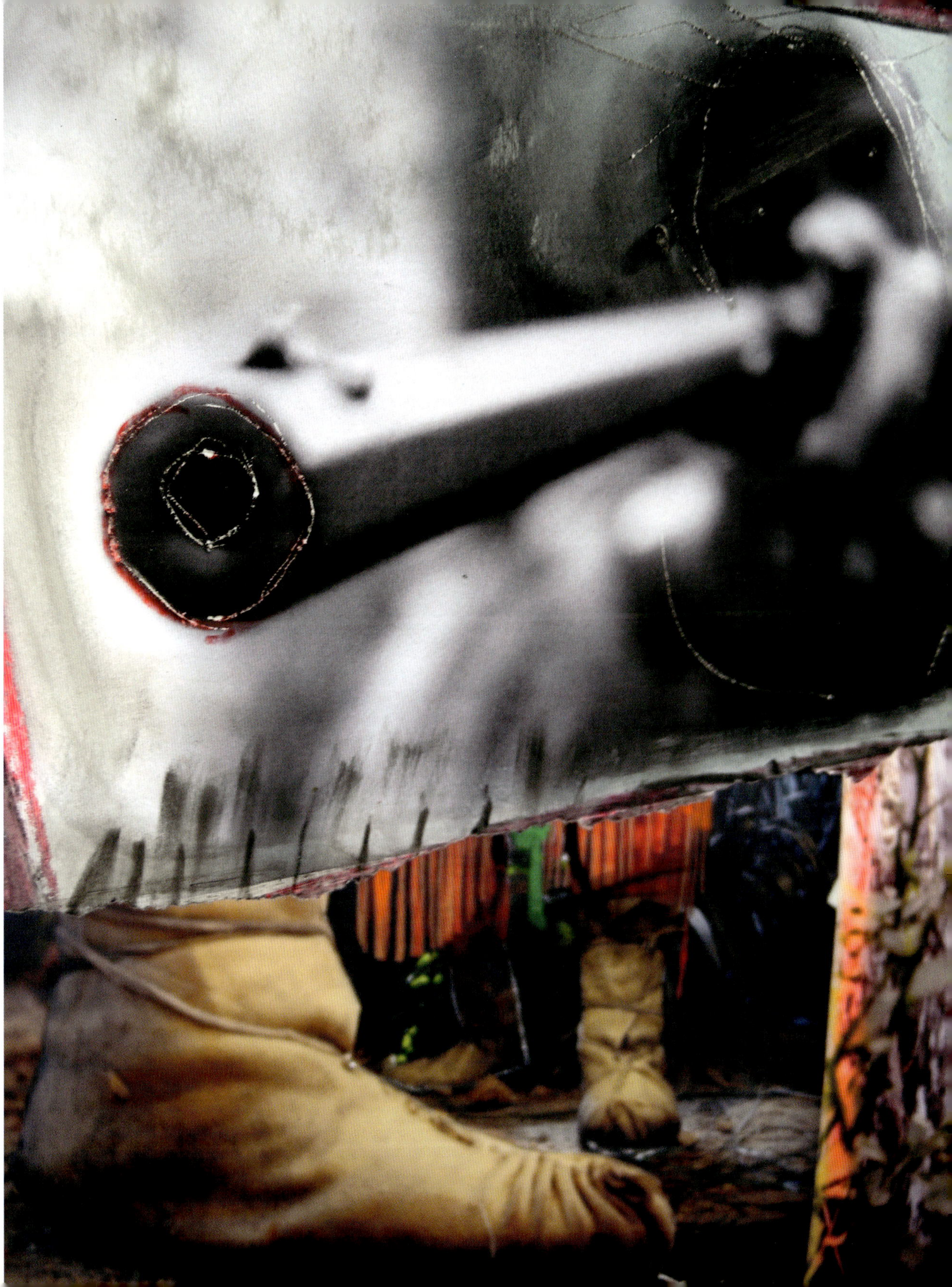

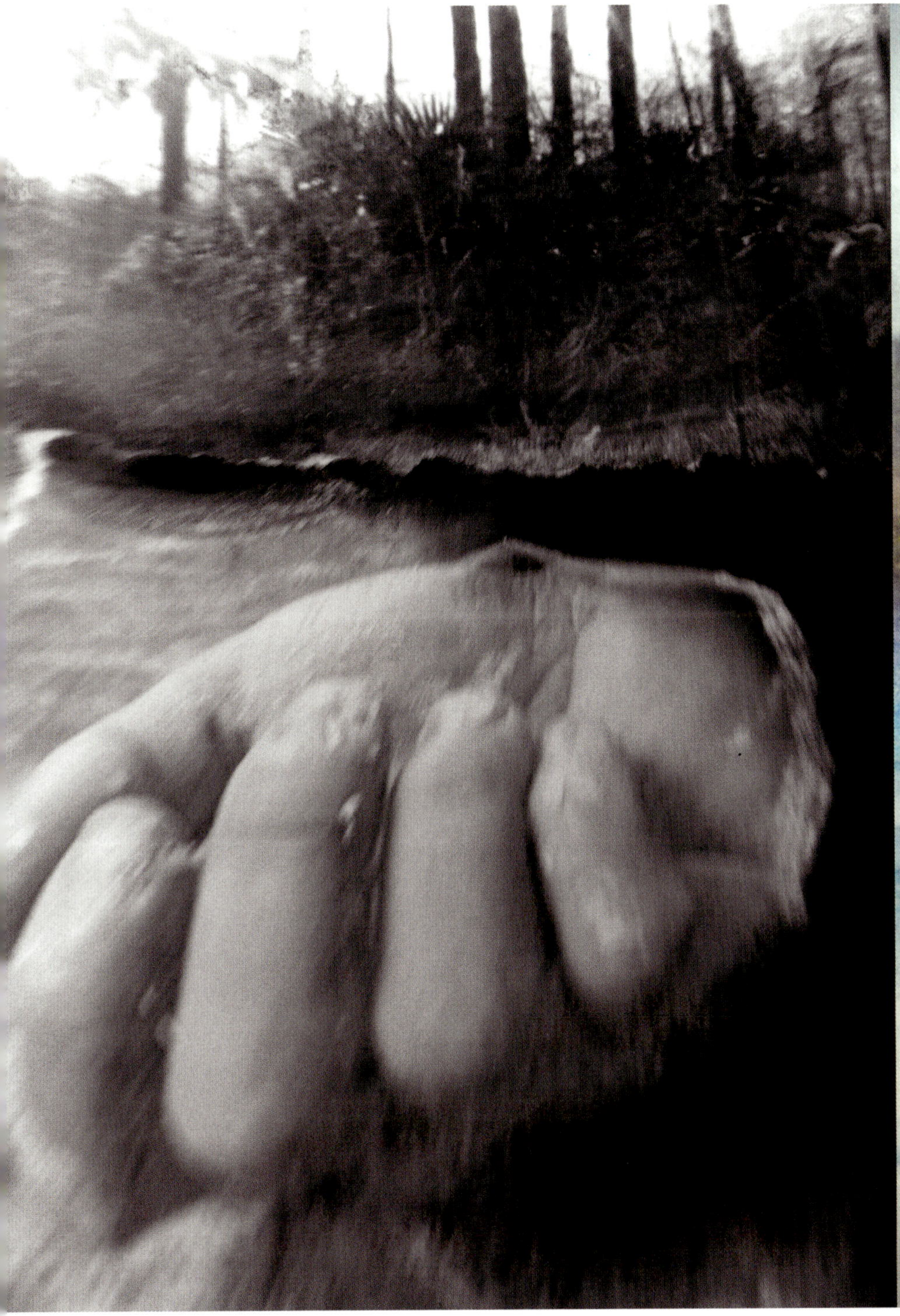
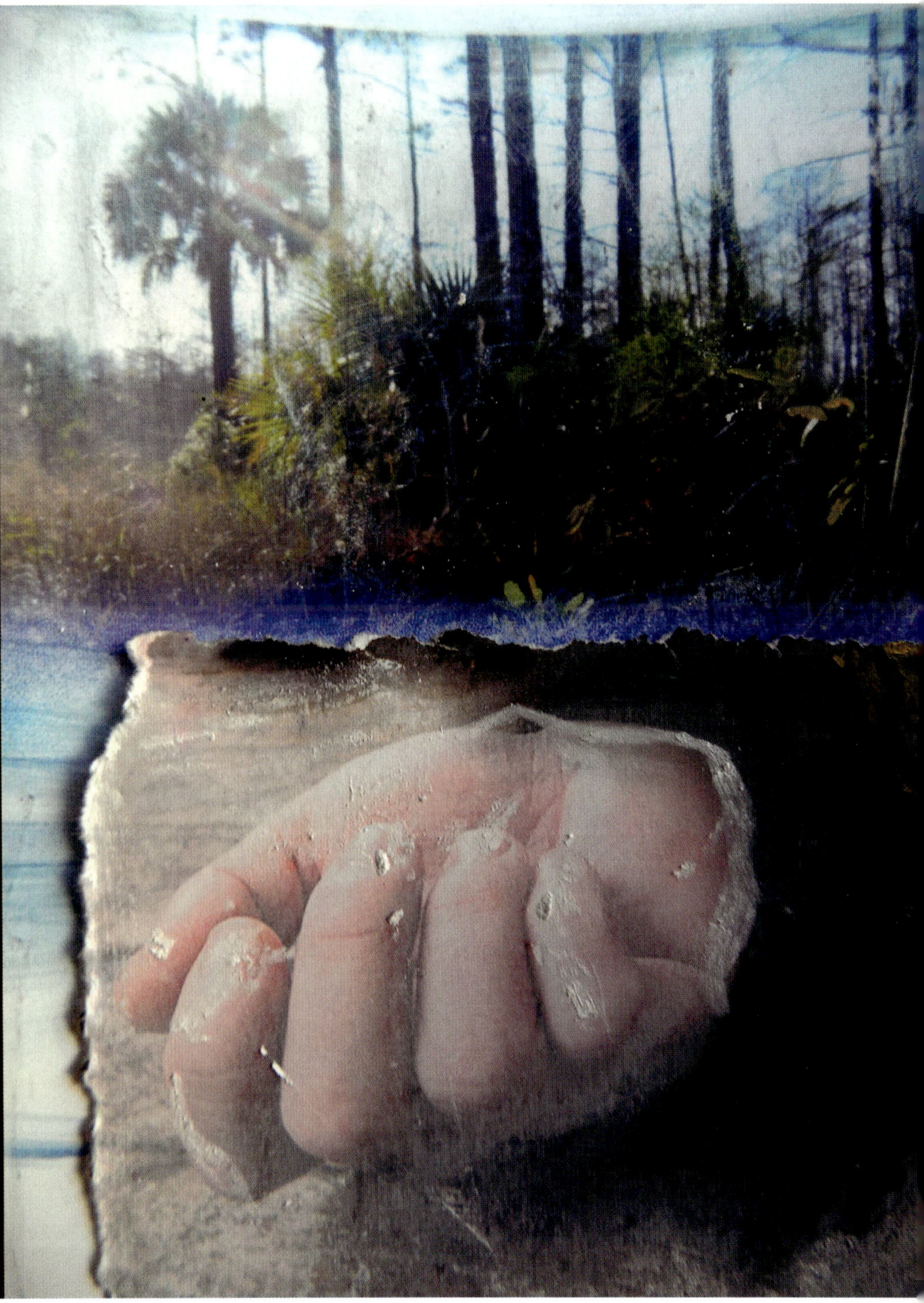

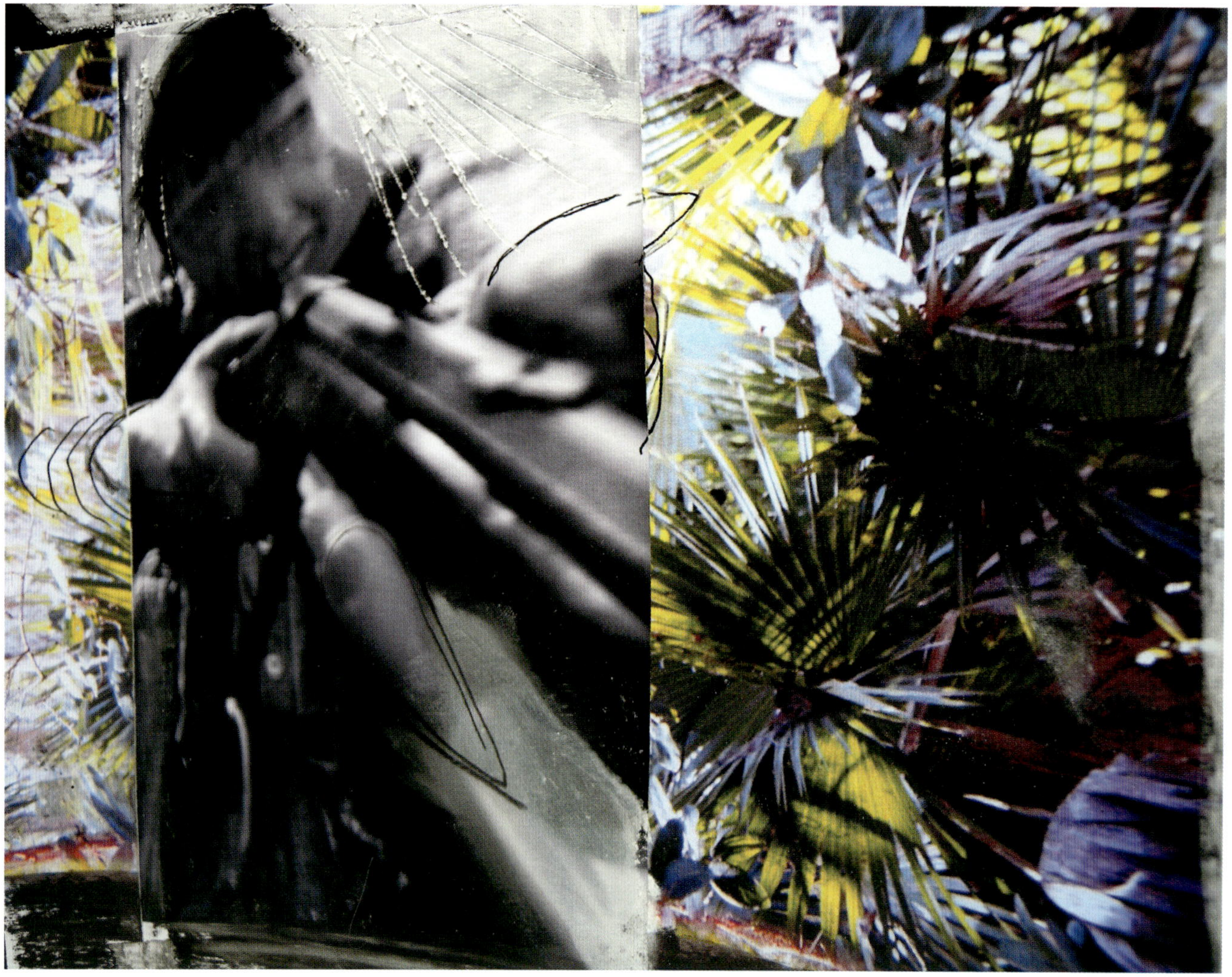

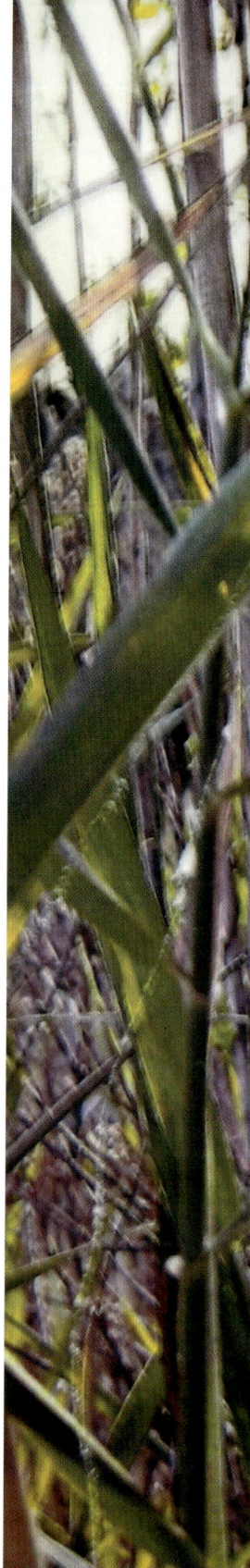

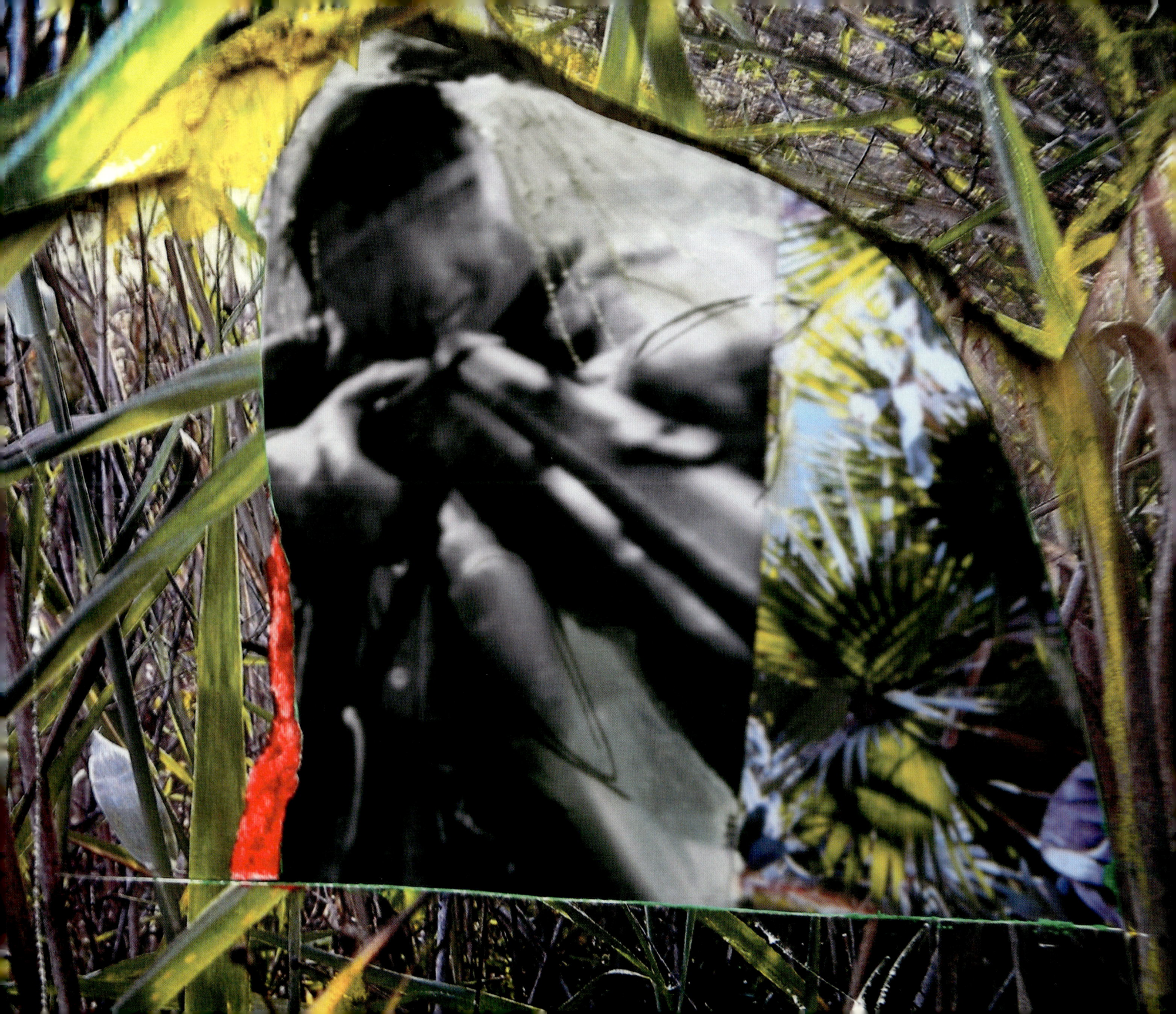

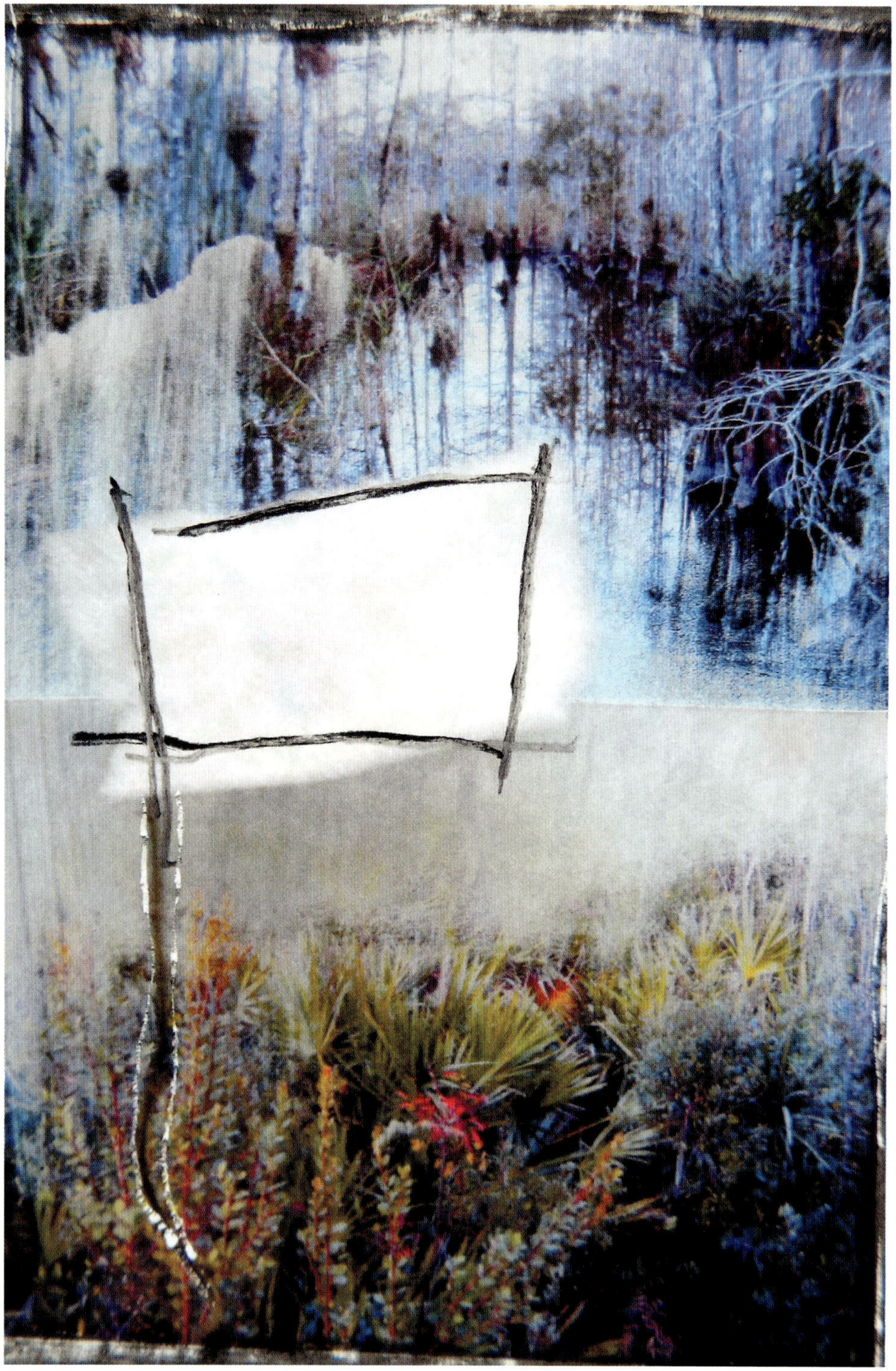

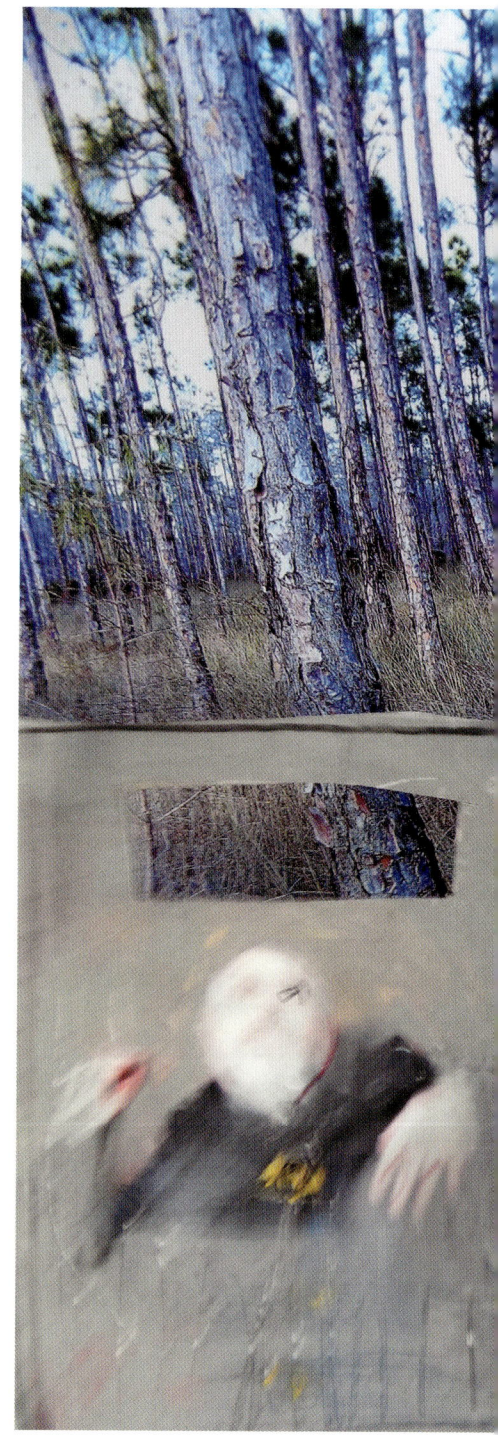

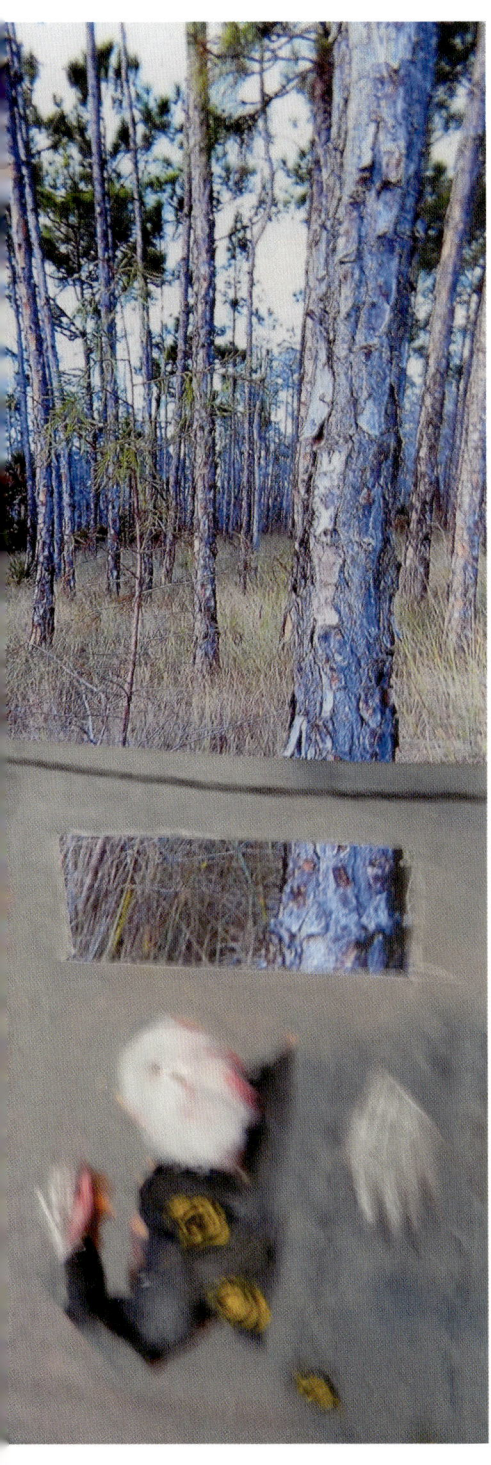

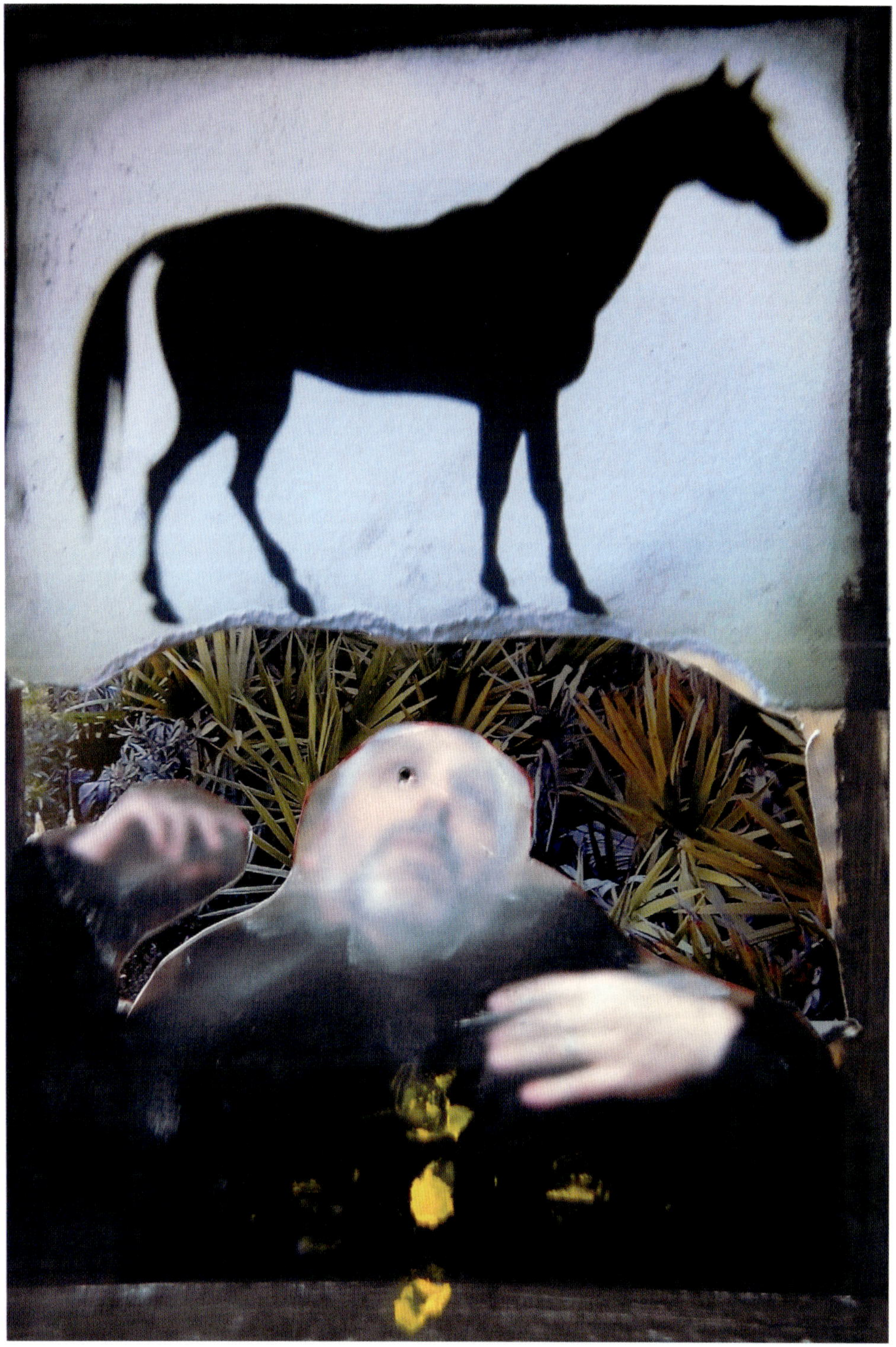

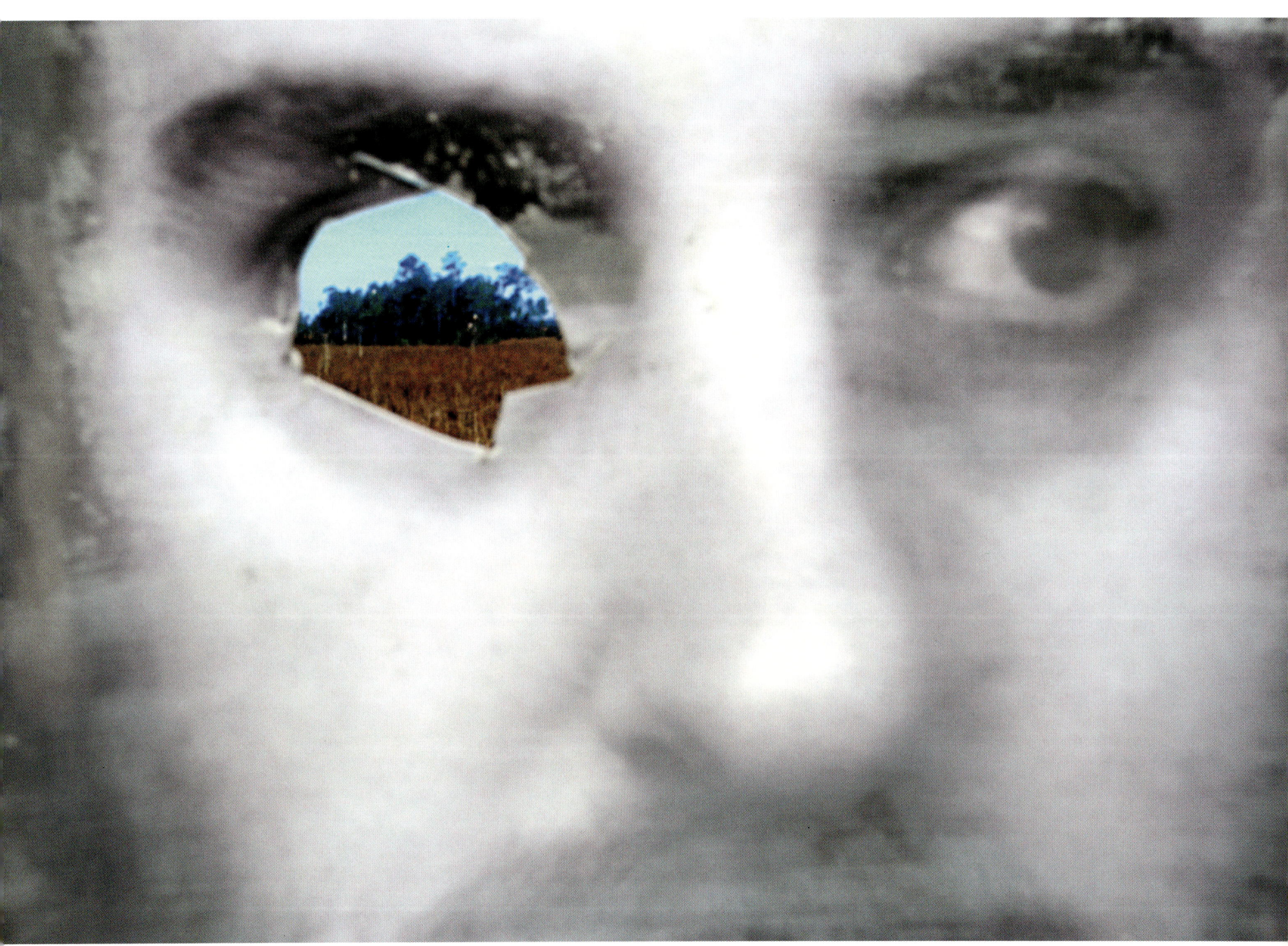

# JIM GOLDBERG & JORDAN STEIN

# Jim Goldberg & Jordan Stein

MAGNUM PHOTOGRAPHER JIM GOLDBERG AND
CURATOR-EDUCATOR JORDAN STEIN HAVE
COLLABORATED ON A DISCOVERY OF THE EVERGLADES
THAT BLURS ANY SENSE OF HIERARCHY AND ACHIEVES
A RELATIVELY HOLISTIC SENSE OF ELEMENTS THAT
ARE AS COMPETITIVE AS THEY ARE COMPLEMENTARY.
THEIR GOAL FOR THE COMMISSION WAS "SIMPLY
TO GET LOST IN THE EXPERIENCE." THE RESULTING
INSTALLATION OF THEIR WORK JUXTAPOSES A
CATALOG OF RESIDENTS FROM THE SOUTHERN
REACHES OF THE EVERGLADES WITH SURVEILLANCE
VIDEOS OF LOCAL WILDLIFE; DOUBLE-SIDED LIGHT
BOXES FEATURING NARRATIVELY POTENT MOMENTS
REFLECT AGAINST PORTABLE LANDSCAPE IMAGES
THAT RANDOMLY LEAN AGAINST THE WALLS; AND A
SUSPENDED AND UPENDED BOAT FLOATS ABOVE THE
ENTIRE SPACE.

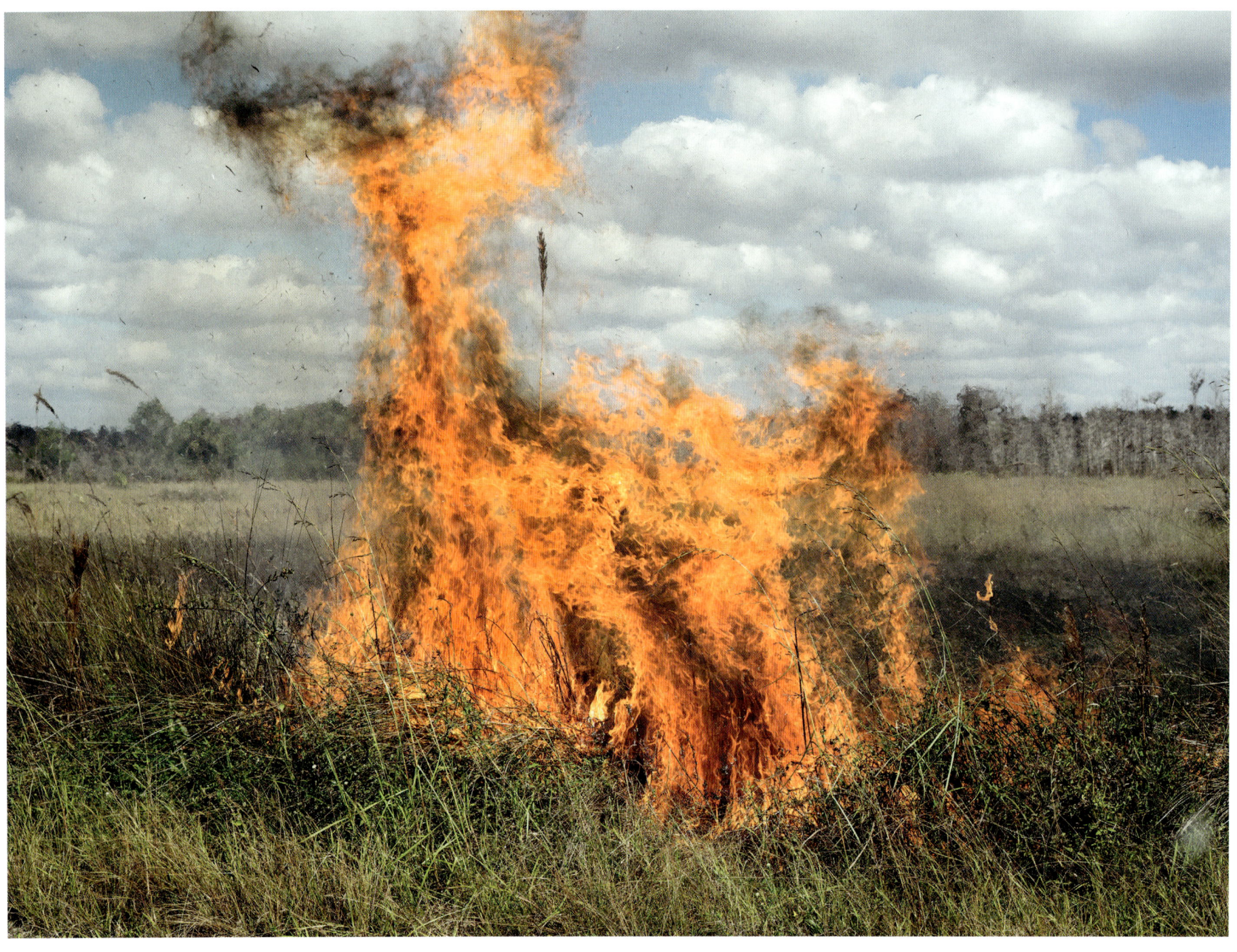

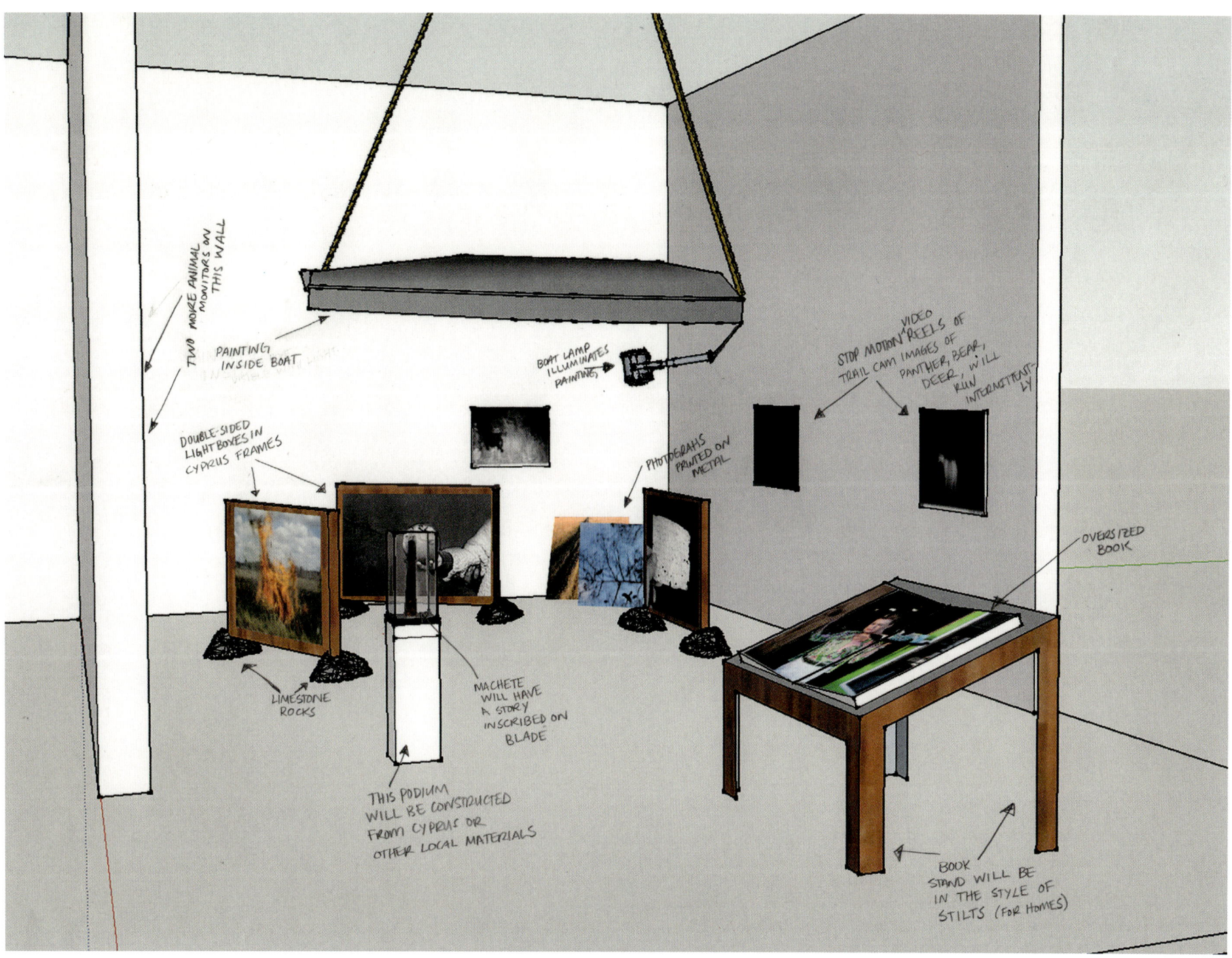

TWO MORE ANIMAL
MONITORS ON
THIS WALL

PAINTING
INSIDE BOAT

BOAT LAMP
ILLUMINATES
PAINTING,

VIDEO
STOP MOTION REELS OF
TRAIL CAM IMAGES OF
PANTHER, BEAR,
DEER, WILL
RUN
INTERMITTENT
LY

DOUBLE-SIDED
LIGHTBOXES IN
CYPRUS FRAMES

PHOTOGRAPHS
PRINTED ON
METAL

OVERSIZED
BOOK

LIMESTONE
ROCKS

MACHETE
WILL HAVE
A STORY
INSCRIBED ON
BLADE

THIS PODIUM
WILL BE CONSTRUCTED
FROM CYPRUS OR
OTHER LOCAL MATERIALS

BOOK
STAND WILL BE
IN THE STYLE OF
STILTS (FOR HOMES)

77

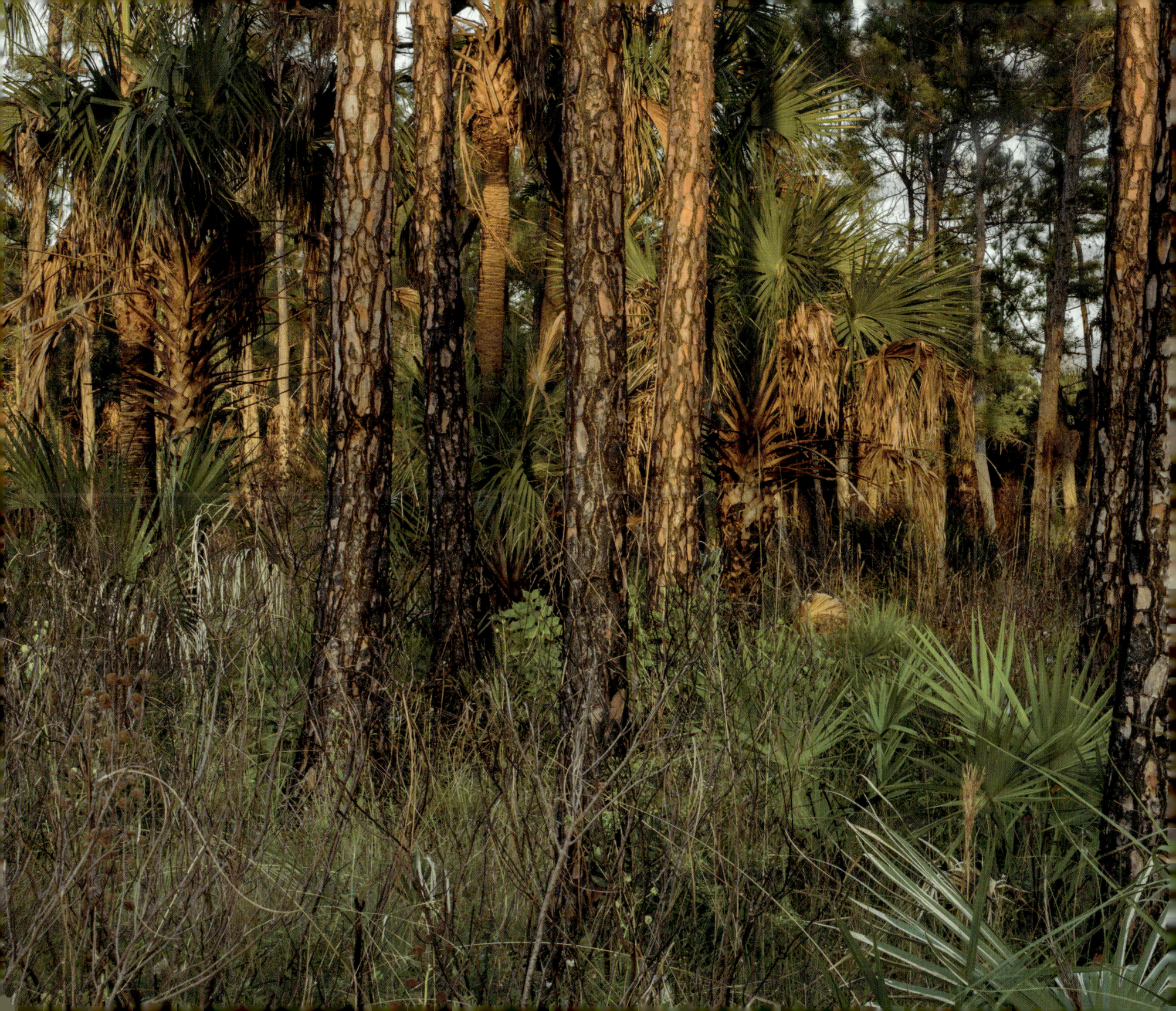

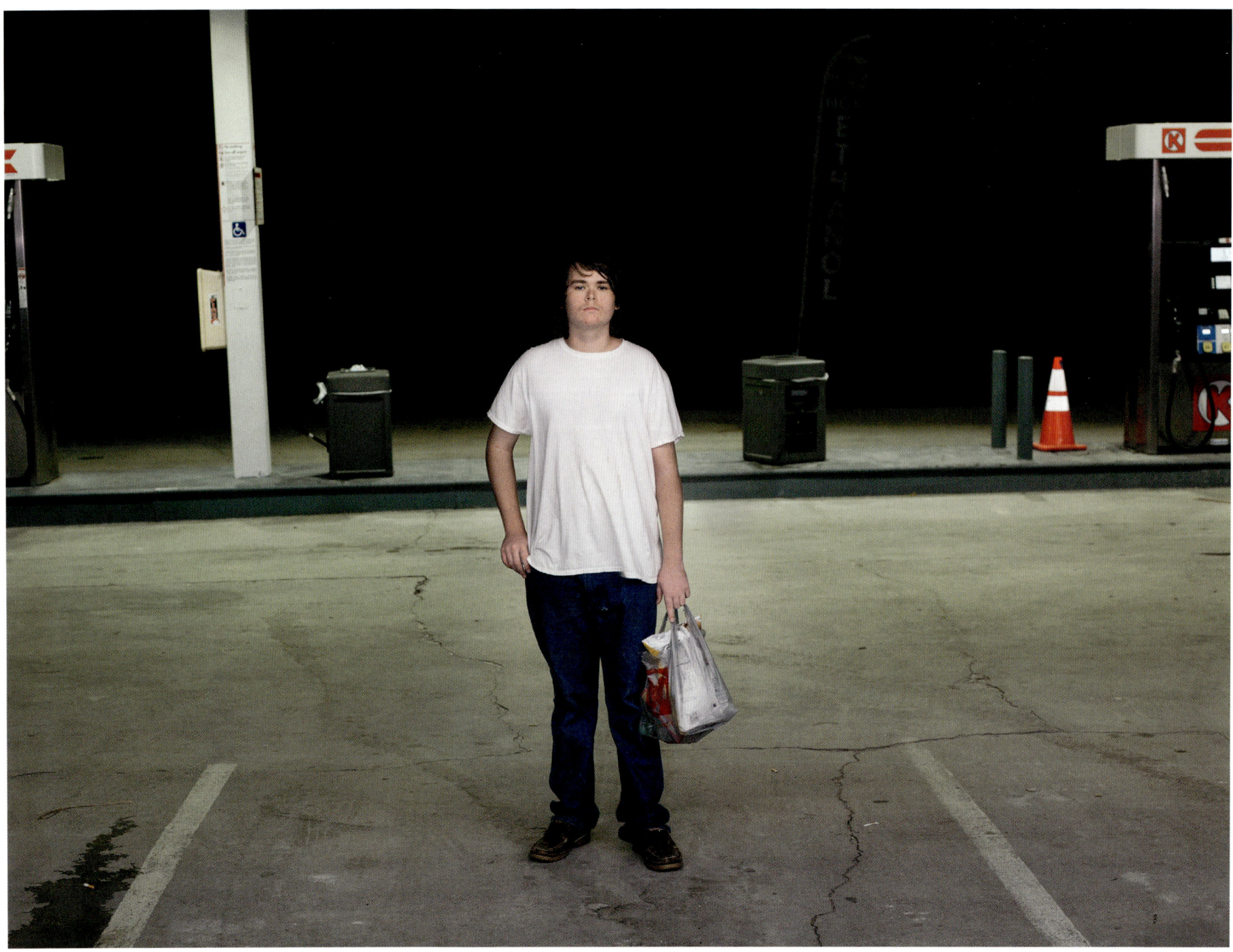

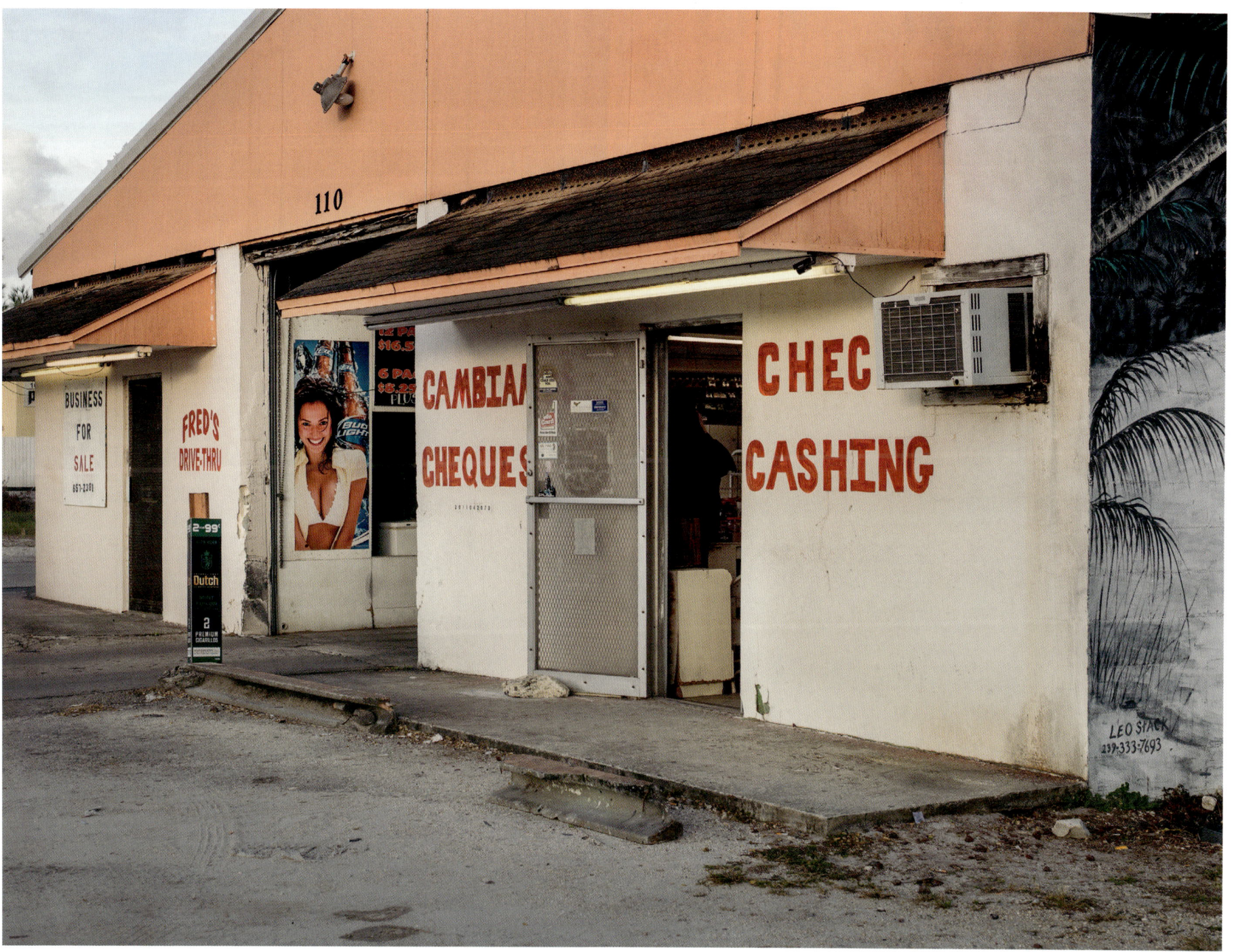

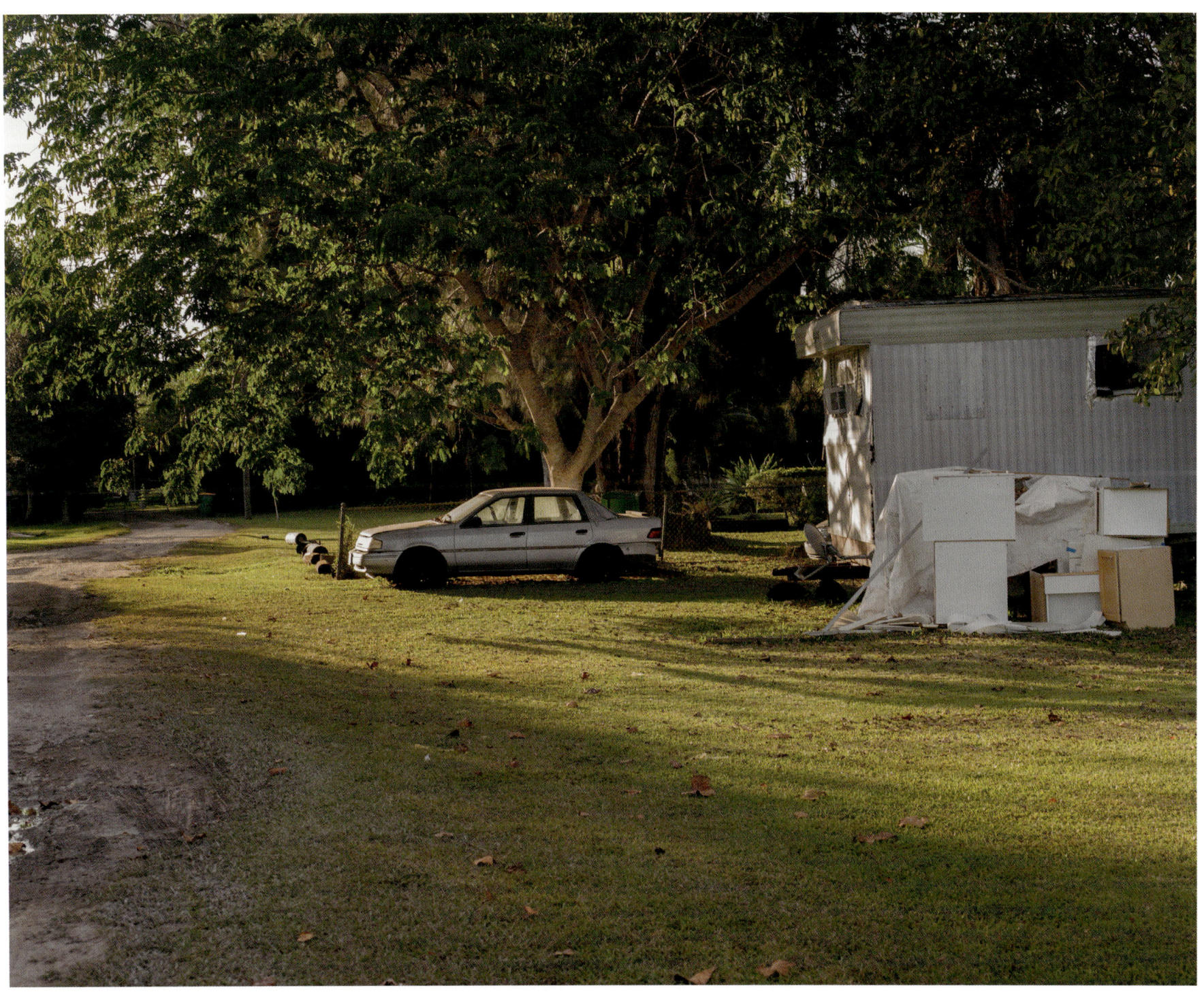

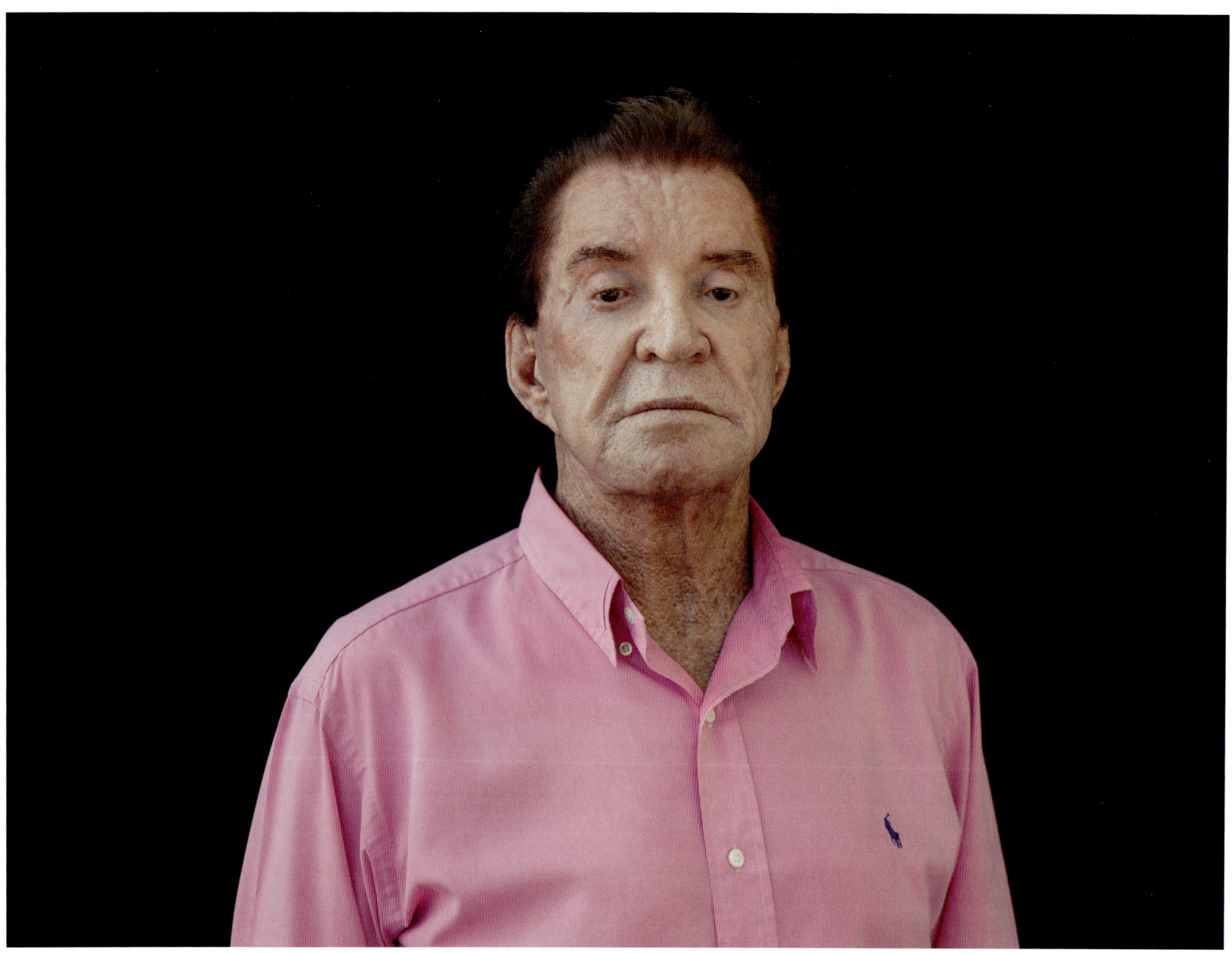

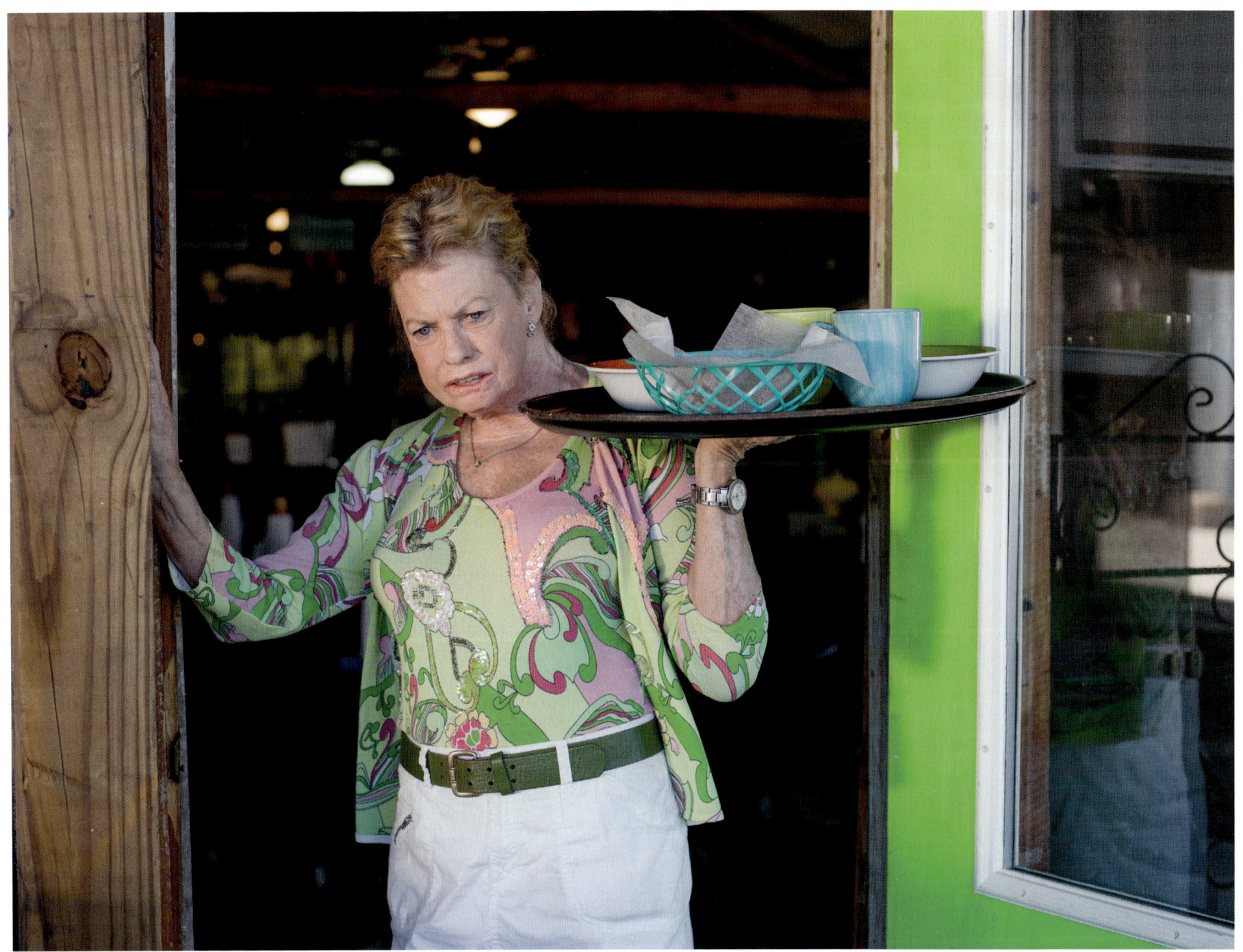

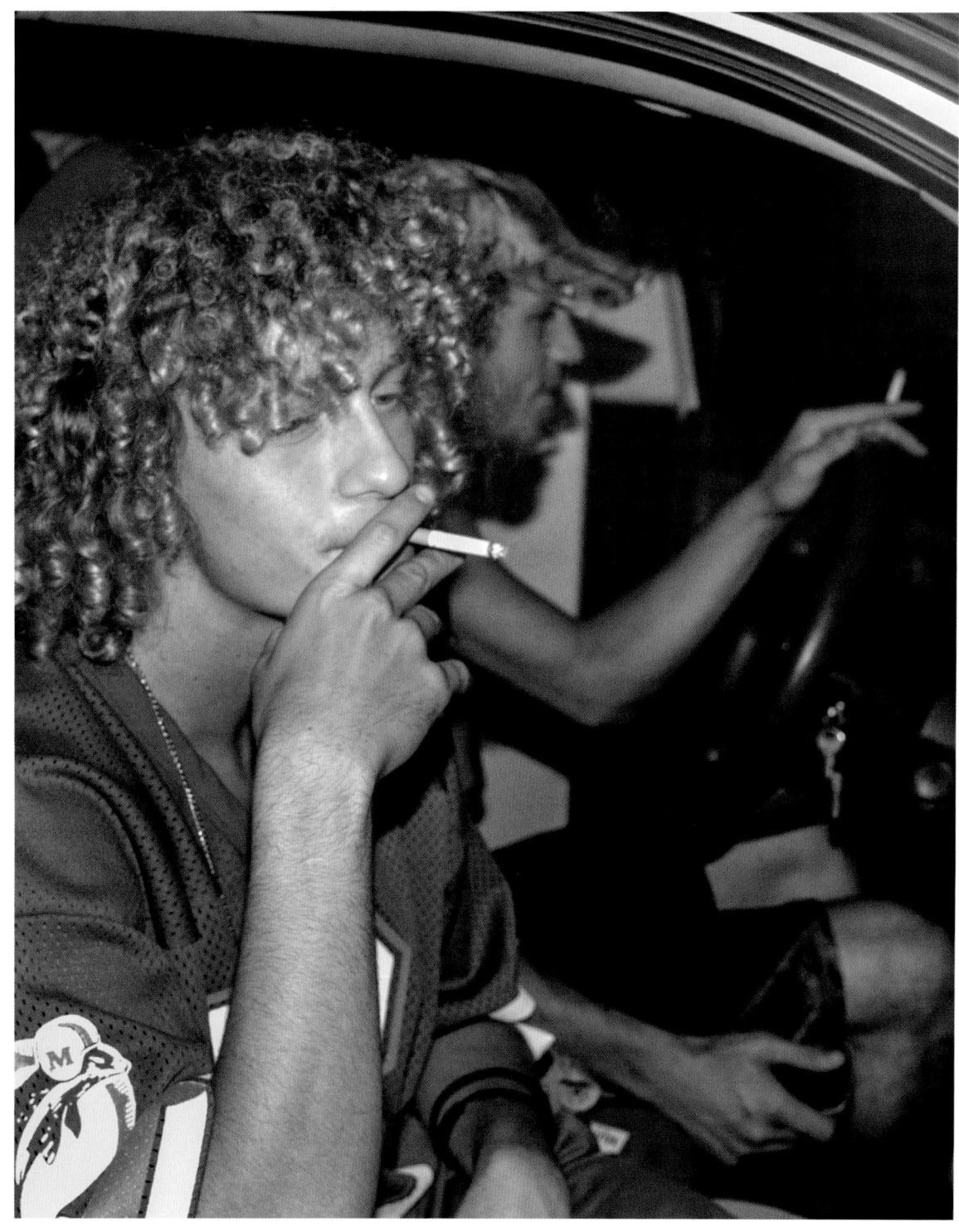

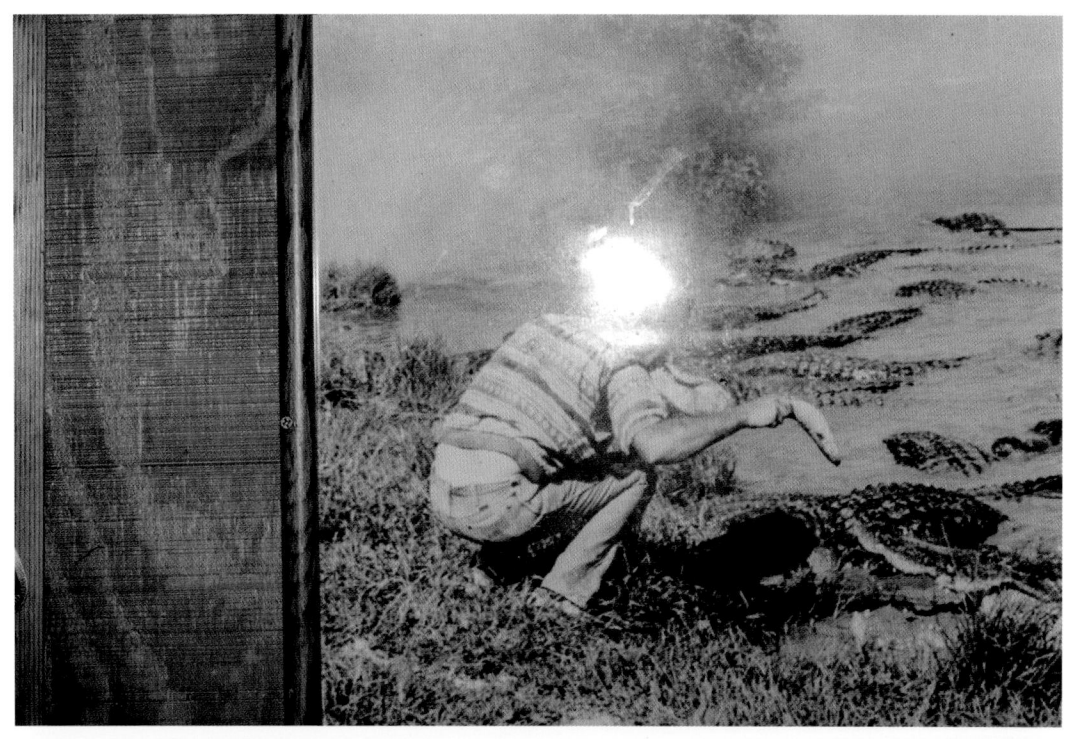

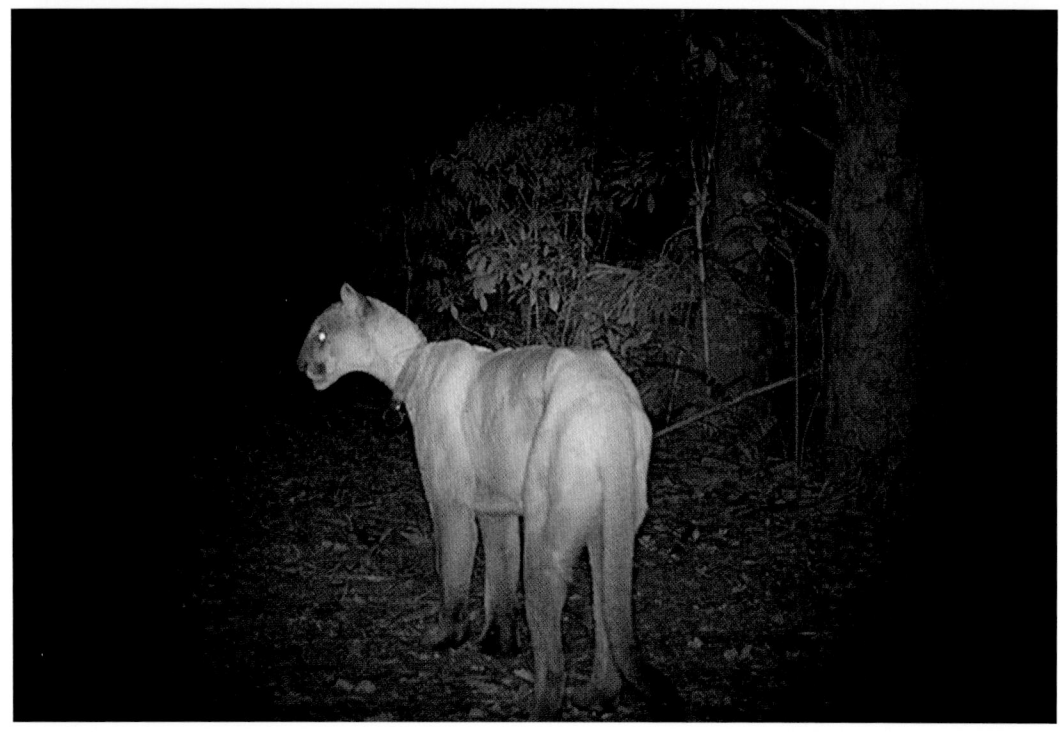

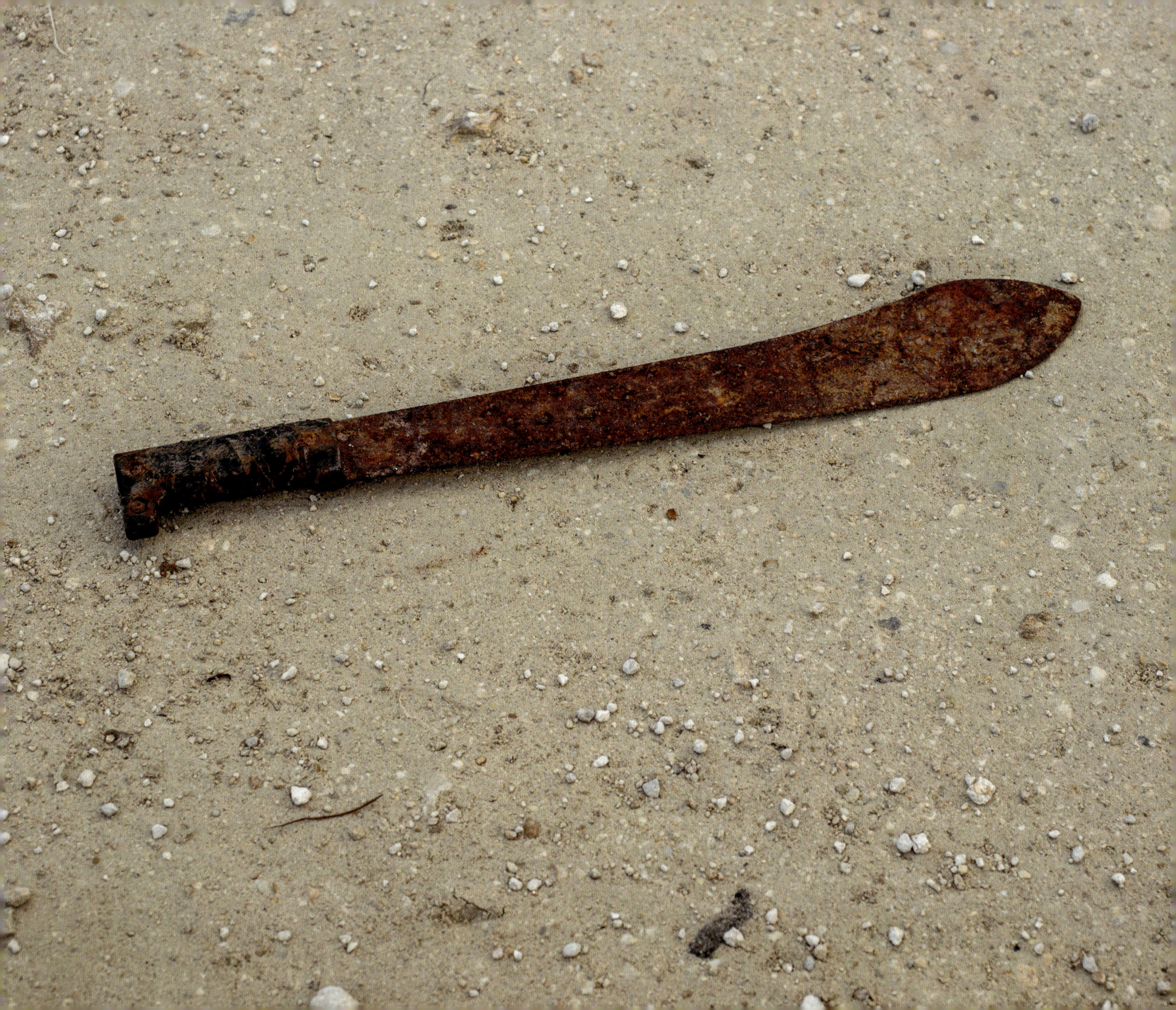

# EXHIBITION CHECKLIST

## Unidentified Photographers

[Group portrait with alligator],
1916–1917
Gelatin silver print
6 ⅞ x 9 ½ in.
Collection of the Lawrence E. Will
Museum of the Glades, Belle Glade, FL

[3 mounted photographs], circa 1925
(3) Gelatin silver prints on board
3 ⅜ x 5 ⅝ in. (image 1)
3 ⅜ x 5 ⅝ in. (image 2)
2 ⅝ x 4 ½ in. (image 3)
Collection of the Lawrence E. Will
Museum of the Glades, Belle Glade, FL

[Clearing custard apple trees], 1920
Gelatin silver print
2 ½ x 4 1/16 in.
Collection of the Lawrence E. Will
Museum of the Glades, Belle Glade, FL

[Dredge Okeechobee], 1908
Gelatin silver print
7 ½ x 9 ½ in.
Collection of the Lawrence E. Will
Museum of the Glades, Belle Glade, FL

[Buckeye Ditcher], undated
Gelatin silver print
2 ⅝ x 4 ⅝ in.
Collection of the Lawrence E. Will
Museum of the Glades, Belle Glade, FL

## William Henry Jackson
## (United States, 1843–1942)

*Deep Creek*, circa 1898, printed later
Gelatin silver print
7 ½ x 9 ½ in.
Norton Museum of Art, Purchase,
R.H. Norton Trust, 83.31

*Mangroves in Jupiter Narrrows*, circa
1889, printed later
Gelatin silver print
7 ½ x 9 ½ in.
Norton Museum of Art, Purchase,
R.H. Norton Trust, 83.4

## Ralph M. Munroe
## (United States, 1851–1933)

*Cypress Charlie's Squaw, Seminole
Indian*, circa 1890, printed later
Gelatin silver print
6 ½ x 8 ½ in.
Norton Museum of Art, Purchase,
R.H. Norton Trust, 83.38

*Dr. Tiger, Seminole Indian*, circa 1890,
printed later
Gelatin silver print
6 ⅛ x 8 ⅛ in.
Norton Museum of Art, Purchase,
R.H. Norton Trust, 83.40

*Ye Noble Red Men, Seminoles*, circa 1890,
printed later
Gelatin silver print
6 ⅛ x 8 ⅛ in.
Norton Museum of Art, Purchase,

R.H. Norton Trust, 83.44

*Old Emanthla, Seminole Indian,
85 years old*, circa 1890, printed later
Gelatin silver print
6 ⅜ x 8 ⅜ in.
Norton Museum of Art, Purchase,
R.H. Norton Trust, 83.42

*Seminoles*, circa 1890, printed later
Gelatin silver print
6 ½ x 8 ⅜ in.
Norton Museum of Art, Purchase,
R.H. Norton Trust, 83.43

## John King Sr.
## (United States, 20th Century)

[In the Glades], 1917
Gelatin silver print
2 ⅜ x 3 in.
Collection of Marilyn Catlow

[In the Glades], 1917
Gelatin silver print
3 x 3 ⅞ in.
Collection of Marilyn Catlow

[Dry slough], 1917
Gelatin silver print
3 x 5 ¼ in.
Collection of Marilyn Catlow

[River view], 1917
Gelatin silver print
3 x 5 ¼ in.
Collection of Marilyn Catlow

[River view], 1917
Gelatin silver print
4 ⅛ x 2 ½ in.
Collection of Marilyn Catlow

[River view], 1917
Gelatin silver print
4 ⅛ x 2 ½ in.
Collection of Marilyn Catlow

[River view], 1917
Gelatin silver print
4 ⅛ x 2 ½ in.
Collection of Marilyn Catlow

[Mangroves], 1917
Gelatin silver print
4 ⅛ x 2 ½ in.
Collection of Marilyn Catlow

[Dense foliage], 1917
Gelatin silver print
4 ⅛ x 2 ½ in.
Collection of Marilyn Catlow

[Gator], 1917
Gelatin silver print
1 ⅝ x 2 in.
Collection of Marilyn Catlow

**Walker Evans**
**(United States, 1903–1975)**

[Cypresses in Swamp, Florida], 1941,
printed ca. 1970
Gelatin silver print
8 11⁄16 x 6 ¾ in.
Lent by the Metropolitan Museum of
Art, Gift of Arnold Crane, 1972
1972.742.27

*Banyan Tree, Florida*, 1941, printed ca.
1970
Gelatin Silver Print
8 13⁄16 x 7 1⁄16 in.
Lent by the Metropolitan Museum of
Art, Gift of Arnold Crane, 1972
1972.742.26

**Marion Post Wolcott**
**(United States, 1910–1990)**

*Migratory Workers' Camp: Single Room
Cabin, Two Dollars a Week; Double
Room Cabin, 4 Dollars; Water Must be
Hauled, Belle Glade*, 1939, printed later
Gelatin silver print
10 ¼ x 13 ⅜ in.
Norton Museum of Art, Purchase,
R.H. Norton Trust, 83.61

*Migrant Agricultural Workers' Shack
Near Lake Okeechobee, FL (Child
in Doorway)*, 1939, printed 1979
Gelatin silver print
7 x 9 in.
Courtesy Joshua Mann Paillet, A
Gallery for Fine Photography, New
Orleans

*Migrant Family from Missouri, Canal
Point, FL*, 1939
Gelatin silver print
6 ¾ x 6 ¾ in.
Courtesy Joshua Mann Paillet, A
Gallery for Fine Photography, New
Orleans

*Pahokee Hotel, Migrant Vegetable
Pickers' Quarters Near Homestead, FL*,
1941, printed 1979
Gelatin silver print
8 ½ x 11 ¼ in.
Courtesy Joshua Mann Paillet, A
Gallery for Fine Photography, New
Orleans

*Two White Couples in Booth in Juke
Joint, Near Morehaven, FL*, 1939
Gelatin silver print
7 x 9 in.
Courtesy Joshua Mann Paillet, A
Gallery for Fine Photography, New
Orleans

**Eliot Porter**
**(United States,1901–1990)**

*Purple Gallinule, Everglades National
Park, Florida, March 2, 1954*, 1954
Dye imbibition print
8 ½ x 10 3⁄16 in.
Amon Carter Museum of American Art,
Fort Worth, Texas, Gift of the artist,
P1989.19.11

*Saw Palmetto, Kissimmee Prairie,
Florida, April 4, 1954*, 1954
Dye imbibition print
8 ½ x 10 ¾ in.
Amon Carter Museum of American Art,
Fort Worth, Texas, Bequest of the artist,
P1990.51.2161

*Cypress Slough and Mist, Cypress Lodge,
Punta Gorda, Florida, January 31, 1974*,
1974
Dye imbibition print
10 ½ x 8 1⁄16 in.
Amon Carter Museum of American Art,
Fort Worth, Texas, Bequest of the artist,
P1990.51.2171.1

*Louisiana Heron, Mrazik Pond,
Everglades National Park, Florida,
January 1974*, 1974
Dye imbibition print
7 5⁄16 x 10 in.
Amon Carter Museum of American Art,
Fort Worth, Texas, Bequest of the artist,
P1990.52.39

*Snowy Egret, Kissimmee Prairie,
Florida, April 1954*, 1954
Dye imbibition print
7 7⁄16 x 10 in.
Amon Carter Museum of American Art,
Fort Worth, Texas, Bequest of the artist,
P1990.52.24.3

*Strangler Fig Roots, Everglades National
Park, Florida, March 7, 1954*, 1954
Dye imbibition print
10 ¾ x 8 7⁄16 in.
Amon Carter Museum of American Art,
Fort Worth, Texas, Gift of the artist,
P1989.19.93

**Clyde Butcher**
**(United States, b. 1942)**

*Thompson Pine Island Road Number
Three*, 1986
Gelatin silver print, edition 16 of 250
10 x 14 in.
Norton Museum of Art, Gift of
Mildred and Herbert Lee, 2000.19

*Moonrise Number Two*, 1986
Gelatin silver print, ed. 20/250
14 x 11 in. (35.6 x 25.4 cm)
Norton Museum of Art, Gift of
Mildred and Herbert Lee, 2000.21

*Rock Island Prairie Number Two*, 1987
Gelatin silver print, ed. 6/250
18 x 24 in.
Norton Museum of Art, Gift of
Mildred and Herbert Lee, 2000.22

*Cigar Orchid Pond #1*, 2009
Gelatin silver print, edition 4 of 50
26 ¾ x 37 ½ in.
Collection of Mr. and Mrs. George
Otto Gratz

## Lisa Elmaleh
### (United States, b. 1984)

*Mangroves*, 2010
(2) Gelatin silver prints
20 x 24 in. (each)
Courtesy of the artist

*Vultures*, 2009
Gelatin silver print
24 x 20 in.
Courtesy of the artist

*Paurotis Palms*, 2010
Gelatin silver print
8 x 10 in.
Courtesy of the artist

*Dwarf Cypress Forest*, 2010
Gelatin silver print
8 x 10 in.
Courtesy of the artist

*Slash Pines Reflected in Pine Glades
Lake*, 2010
Gelatin silver print
8 x 10 in.
Courtesy of the artist

*Slash Pines Reflected in Pine Glades
Lake*, 2010
Wet-collodion, glass-plate negative
8 x 10 in.
Courtesy of the artist

*Roots (intestines)*, 2011
Gelatin silver print
8 x 10 in.
Courtesy of the artist

## James Balog
### (United States, b. 1952)

*Florida Panther*, 1989
Chromogenic development print
48 x 48 in.
Norton Museum of Art, Purchase,
R.H. Norton Trust in memory of Dee
Snyder, 92.28

*Brown Pelican*, 1989
Chromogenic development print
48 x 48 in.
Norton Museum of Art, Purchase,
R.H. Norton Trust in memory of Dee
Snyder, 92.27

*Green Sea Turtle*, 1989
Chromogenic development print
48 x 48 in.
Purchase, R.H. Norton Trust in
memory of Dee Snyder, 92.29

## Mary Peck
### (United States, b. 1954)

*Everglades, Snake Bight*, 1986
Gelatin silver print, edition 2/25
11 ⅛ x 30 ½ in.
Norton Museum of Art, Purchase,
William and Sarah Ross Soter
Photography Fund, 2014.77

*Everglades*, 1988
Gelatin silver print, edition 8/25
11 ⅛ x 30 ½ in.
Norton Museum of Art, Purchase,
William and Sarah Ross Soter
Photography Fund, 2014.80

*Everglades*, 1988
Gelatin silver print, edition 4/25
11 ⅛ x 30 ½ in.
Norton Museum of Art, Purchase,
William and Sarah Ross Soter
Photography Fund, 2014.81

*Everglades* [coastline], 1986
Gelatin silver print, edition 7/25
11 ⅛ x 30 ½ in.
Norton Museum of Art, Purchase,
William and Sarah Ross Soter
Photography Fund, 2014.79

*Everglades*, 1986
Gelatin silver print, edition 6/25
11 ⅛ x 30 ½ in.
Norton Museum of Art, Purchase,
William and Sarah Ross Soter
Photography Fund, 2014.82

## Adam Nadel
### (United States, b. 1967)

*Non-Native Seminole War Re-enactor,
Second Seminole War Reenactment, Big
Cypress Reservation, FL*, 2014
from the series "Getting the
Water Right"
Archival pigment print, artist's proof
29 ½ x 29 ¾ in.
Norton Museum of Art, Purchased
with funds provided by the William
and Sarah Ross Soter Photography
Fund, 2015.

*Deceased Union Soldier Re-enactors,
Second Seminole War Reenactment, Big
Cypress Reservation, FL*, 2014
from the series "Getting the
Water Right"
Archival pigment print, artist's proof
29 ½ x 29 ¾ in.
Norton Museum of Art, Purchase,
William and Sarah Ross Soter
Photography Fund, 2015.

*Sugar Cane Field Burn, Northeast of
Belle Glade*, 2013
from the series "Getting the
Water Right"
Archival pigment print, artist's proof
29 ¾ x 29 ¾ in.
Courtesy of the artist

*South Florida Water Management
District (SFWMD) Control Room,
South Palm Beach, FL*, 2013
from the series "Getting the
Water Right"

Archival pigment print, artist's proof
29 ½ x 29 ½ in.
Courtesy of the artist

*Lee Thompson, Pump Station,*
*Everglades Agricultural Area, FL*, 2013
from the series "Getting the
Water Right"
Archival pigment print, artist's proof
29 ¾ x 29 ¾ in.
Courtesy of the artist

*Diorama, Southern Florida Museum,*
*Bradenton, FL*, 2013
from the series "Getting the
Water Right"
Archival pigment print, artist's proof
29 ¾ x 29 ¾ in.
Courtesy of the artist

*Herbert Hoover Dike, Southern Rim of*
*Lake Okeechobee, FL*, 2012
from the series "Getting the
Water Right"
Archival pigment print, artist's proof
29 ¾ x 29 ¾ in.
Courtesy of the artist

*Pump, Everglades Restoration Facility,*
*FL*, 2014
from the series "Getting the
Water Right"
Archival pigment print, artist's proof
29 ¾ x 29 ¾ in.
Courtesy of the artist

**Bryan Wilson**
**(United States, b. 1992)**

*Flag of the Land*, 2013
from the series "The Great
American Python"
Embroidery on denim
20 in x 24 in.
Courtesy of the Artist

*Cesar on Patrol*, 2013
from the series "The Great
American Python"
Archival pigment print
20 x 16 in.
Courtesy of the Artist

*Tom with Tool*, 2013
from the series "The Great
American Python"
Archival pigment print
16 x 20 in.
Courtesy of the artist

*Great American Python*, 2013
from the series "The Great
American Python"
Watercolor and ink on paper.
16 x 12 in.
Courtesy of the artist

*Double Snake*, 2013
from the series "The Great
American Python"
Archival pigment print
14 x 11 in.
Courtesy of the artist

*Ouruboros*, 2013
from the series "The Great
American Python"
Archival pigment print
14 x 11 in.
Courtesy of the Artist

**Christy Gast**
**(United States, b. 1979)**

*Herbert Hoover Dyke*, 2010
Video projection
14:45
Courtesy of the artist

**Dana Levy**
**(Israel, b. 1989)**

*Everglades*, 2014
Single channel video
6:50 min
Courtesy of the artist and Braverman
Gallery, Tel Aviv

**Jerry Burchfield**
**(United States, 1947–2009)**

*Toxidendron radicans (Poison Ivy)*, 2008
(4) Lumen prints
20 x 16 in. (each)
Southeast Museum of Photography,
Daytona State College

*Serena Repens (Saw Palmetto)*, 2008
(4) Lumen prints
20 x 16 in. (each)

Southeast Museum of Photography,
Daytona State College

*Asimina obovata (Pawpaw)*, 2007
Lumen print
10 x 8 in.
Southeast Museum of Photography,
Daytona State College

*Pinus elliottii (Slash Pine)*, 2008
Lumen print
20 x 16 in.
Southeast Museum of Photography,
Daytona State College

# CONTEMPORARY COMMISSIONS

**Jim Goldberg**
(United States, b. 1952)
**Jordan Stein**
(United States, b. 1979)

*Everglades*, 2015
Site-specific installation incorporating,
photography, video, artifacts, rock,
metal and wood.
23 x 16 x 10 ft. (overall)
Courtesy of the artists, Commissioned
by the Norton Museum of Art

**Jungjin Lee**
(Korea, b. 1961)

*Everglades 18* [black bird], 2014
from the series "Everglades"
Archival pigment print
28 x 54 ½ in.
Courtesy of the artist, Commissioned
by the Norton Museum of Art.

*Everglades 17* [cloud], 2014
from the series "Everglades"
Archival pigment print
15 x 56 in.
Courtesy of the artist, Commissioned
by the Norton Museum of Art.

*Everglades 02* [bushes], 2014
from the series "Everglades"
Archival pigment print
22 x 77 in.
Courtesy of the artist, Commissioned
by the Norton Museum of Art.

*Everglades 03* [aerial triptych], 2014
from the series "Everglades"
Archival pigment print
28 x 45 in.
Courtesy of the artist, Commissioned
by the Norton Museum of Art.

*Everglades 01* [anhinga triptych], 2014
from the series "Everglades"
Archival pigment print
22 x 144 in.
Courtesy of the artist, Commissioned
by the Norton Museum of Art.

*Everglades 14* [lone tree], 2014
from the series "Everglades"
Archival pigment print
19 x 37 in.
Courtesy of the artist, Commissioned
by the Norton Museum of Art

*Everglades 19* [zigzag tree], 2014
from the series "Everglades"
Archival pigment print
28 x 70 in.
Courtesy of the artist, Commissioned
by the Norton Museum of Art.

**Gerald Slota**
(United States, b. 1965)

*The Second and Third Seminole Wars*,
2015
Archival pigment print installation
8 x 18 ft. (overall)
Courtesy of the artist, Commissioned
by the Norton Museum of Art.

**Bert Teunissen**
**(Netherlands, b. 1959)**

*Sugar Cane Fires*, 2014
(10) Gelatin silver prints
5 ⅝ x 8 ½ in. (each)
Courtesy of the Artist, Commissioned
by the Norton Museum of Art

*A Man Who Wonders*, 2014
(2) Gelatin silver prints
10 ¼ x 13 ⅛ in. (each)
Courtesy of the Artist, Commissioned
by the Norton Museum of Art

*Light Reflections on Sugar Cane, Tree
Leaves, and Alligators*, 2014
(9) Gelatin silver prints
5 ⅞ x 10 ⅝ in. (each)
Courtesy of the Artist, Commissioned
by the Norton Museum of Art

*On the Road*, 2014
(80) Gelatin silver prints
(70) 6 x 4 in. (each)
(10) 7 x 5 in. (each)
Courtesy of the Artist, Commissioned
by the Norton Museum of Art

*Domestic Landscapes. Everglades*, 2014
(29) Archival pigment prints
8 ¼ x 10 ¾ in. (each)
Courtesy of the Artist, Commissioned
by the Norton Museum of Art

# ACKNOWLEDGMENTS

As if in proof of the adage that there are no believers more rabid than the converted, I want to thank the Norton Museum of Art's executive director, Hope Alswang, and trustee Bruce Gendelman, who became the project's most strident ambassadors, deflecting questions of both the relevance and suitability of the Everglades as a subject for an exhibition.

I am fortunate to be able to rely upon Sally and Bill Soter, who are a constant source of grounding and stability and are unflagging in their support—regardless of where I seem to take them. Thanks are due to Muriel and Ralph Saltzman, whose support of the Norton's exhibition program is a model for any museum; to Beth Dowdle and the Board of the Chastain Foundation, whose early seed money was instrumental in seeing this project succeed; and to the National Endowment for the Arts for the validation and authority their support imparts. Lastly, the ongoing support of the members of the Norton's Photography Committee while this project gestated cannot be overstated.

The staff and volunteers of the Norton Museum of Art, past as well as present, are constant sources of encouragement and support. From the back door to the front, from the loading dock to the roof, from the galleries to storage, my colleagues and cohorts are a pleasure to work with and a wonder to behold.

So many people have played a part in the conception, research, and formulation of this exhibition that simple gratitude seems so paltry, yet that is all I can offer to researcher and guide Sarah Brown; David Scheinbaum and Janet Russek; the staff and board of the Everglades Foundation; Gary Lickle and Mary Morse of Chilton Trust; the staff, board, and artists of the AIRIE (Artists in Residence in the Everglades) Foundation and program; and Michael Itkoff, Taj Forer, and Ursula Damm of Daylight Books.

The exhibition would not be possible without the confidence of the many lenders who made their works available: George and Diana Gantz, Rex Hamilton and Béryl Lacoste Hamilton, Joshua Mann Pailet at A Gallery for Fine Photography in New Orleans, and the staffs of the Jupiter Lighthouse Historical Museum, the Glades Museum, the Metropolitan Museum of Art, and most especially, John Rohrbach and the staff at the Amon Carter Museum of American Art. But perhaps most important has been the creativity, energy, and ideas from the artists in the exhibition, whose work both inspired and led me along the way

No one is able to devote three years to a project without having it impact relationships and friendships. I have been fortunate to be surrounded by many who have endured too many facts, too much silence, and too many uncertainties. My thanks to Matt, Brian, Debbie, Rachel, and Samantha Redman; Charlie Stainback and Kitty Bowe Hearty; Eileen Cowin and Jay Brecker; Selma Holo and Fred Croton; Richard delle Fave and Eric Holmgren; Scott Robertson and Jim Swope; and, Bill Hunt and Alec Treuhaft.

Finally, I offer a triple dedication: first to Hilary Jordan and Dak Patriarca, without whom this entire project would not have found its legs; next to Kiki, Ceci, and Jack Welter (and their parents), who have recharged my hopes for the future; and finally, to my friend and colleague Karen Sinsheimer, whose work and life prove that grace under pressure is not an illusion.

*Tim B. Wride, 2015*